Make My Life A Bible

Miracles Do Happen

by

John Taylor

The Praying Cowboy

with

Robin White

Copyright © 2013 by John Taylor and Robin White

Make My Life A Bible
Miracles Do Happen
by John Taylor and Robin White

Printed in the United States of America

ISBN 9781626977464

All rights reserved. Except as permitted under the U.S. Copyright Act of 1976, no part of this publication may be reproduced, distributed, or transmitted in any form or by any means, or stored in a database or retrieval system, without the prior written permission of the publisher.

Unless otherwise indicated, Bible quotations are taken from the King James version of the Bible.

John Taylor
PO Box 644
Kountze, TX 77625

Cover design by Jonathan Fawcett
Photograph on the cover by Jamie Barton

www.xulonpress.com

Table of Contents

Foreward	xv
Introduction	xvii
Make My Life a Bible	21
Lord, I Want MY Life to be Like a Bible	22
The Holy Spirit in My Truck	23
Brain Tumor	26
Breast Cancer	28
Trip to Heaven's gate	29
A Child's Boil	31
Jaw Pain	32
The Muslim and My Cancer	34
Rocks, Oil and Healing	36
How Prayers are Answered	39
Catholic Radio Miracles	42
The Healing Inside the Womb	44
It can Happen to You too	46
The Wound that only He can Heal	48
Healed From Drugs	50
The Bulldozer and Cancer	51
The Power of Praise	52
The Lord can Work in a Funny Way	53
You And I Need Prayer	55
The Miracle of the Oil	57

Anointing Oil and Hurricane Money 60
The Home the Hurricane Spared 64
Healing is Useless without Salvation 65
SINNER'S PRAYER 67
The Hitchhiker 70
Aggie and the Angel 72
Mistreated as a Child 74
Prayer Posse for Jesus 76
All Their Prayers Answered 77
Eight Polygraph Truths 78
Miracles Continue 83
God Rewards Faithfulness 87
The Holy Spirit 91
The Healing Power of God 99
God Uses Doctors 103
About John Taylor 109
Word from the Co-Author 113
About the Cowboy, Horse and the Cross 117
Taylor Tot 121

John & Connie Taylor

I am married to the most wonderful man in the world. He has been a great husband and father to our children. I ask God all the time, to let me be the woman that will be an asset to him and his ministry. I support him one hundred percent. I have often told him that if I didn't live with him and see firsthand so many of these miracles that God has done for His people, I would find it hard to believe. I thank God every day that He has us together. No woman could ask for more. God has given us so many blessings. Blessings as a mortal, I certainly don't deserve. I praise God and thank Him for my wonderful husband and children, family and friends. He has taken me off of my death bed twice in my life. I only want to be worthy enough to enter into Heaven. I tell John if he gets to Heaven before I do, to wait at the gate for me.

Connie Taylor

John sent me a music video of a precious lady with a powerful anointing. We had never met, but his heart was to help the lady reach more people for Jesus. He had seen our Christian television program and wanted to know if we would have her on the show and play her music. We did; she and her music blessed many. John is all about helping people and praying for people. We became friends and I had him on television, sharing his testimony and praying for folks. He has given away over five thousand DVD's of that program and people have accepted Jesus all over America. The world needs more John Taylor's. We are proud to call him friend.

Tommy Thomas, Television and Radio Producer
President of the Light of Life Ministries International
www.HowToBeatTheOdds.com

Cotton Candy Church was a song inspired by John Taylor, a close friend of myself and Cary. First, let me introduce John Taylor. John is a little less than seven feet tall, but not much less. He is a too tall Texas Cowboy. A John Wayne on steroids and he is the biggest cry baby you have ever seen. Well, perhaps I over exaggerate how tall he is, but he is a very gentle giant of a Christian. He loves the Lord and when called will drop everything and go anywhere to pray for anybody at any time. This man is a prayer warrior for Christ. Let me see if I can put that in perspective for you. He is like Genghis Khan for his fearlessness, Atilla the Hun for his wisdom, and General Swartzkoff for compassion for his fellow soldier rolled into one. He is armed with the power of the Holy Spirit as his weapon of choice. We affectionately call him crying John because he can never talk about Jesus without feeling the Holy Spirit and coming to tears. He is such a willing vessel and seriously will stop, drop, and roll to anywhere God moves him to go. John has witnessed untold miracles that have defied mortal logic time and time again. Back to the song, *Cotton Candy Church*. John has dropped into many churches for a visit. Well, John decided to visit this one particular church and it left him wanting. Apparently, it was a "feel good church" where everything is "fine" and "sugar coated." He called it a cotton candy church. And of course singer and song writer Cary Gilham took this and knocked it out of the park with the lyrics. The CD was recorded in a studio along with other unreleased songs for special purposes and intended for a smaller audience.

Perry Weeks

Foreward

When I was asked to do the foreword for John Taylor's book, *Make My Life a Bible*, I was very excited because I personally know his testimony and many of his praise reports. John's life makes you realize Jehovah Rapha is still in the healing business today and that He is working through him, His humble servant.

I believe this book is destined to be a classic. It simplifies the many healing powers of the great Physician. It also leaves you with the reality that healing is happening today for anyone who calls on the name of Jesus.

John's servant hood is precious. He has that childlike faith for those God has assigned him to pray for. When you read how God uses this man it will increase your faith and give you a great hope and encouragement in the living God.

I have confidence this book will greatly impact your life. I encourage you to purchase extra ones to give to people who need a fresh visit of God's healing power.

Dr. Jonie' Dodgens' Ministry
President

Walking with Pawpaw

I like to walk with Pawpaw
His steps are short like mine.
He doesn't say "Now hurry up!"
He always takes his time.
Most people have to hurry.
They do not stop and see.
I'm glad that God made Pawpaw.
"Unrushed" and young like me.
Love Taylor Tot

Introduction

I met John Taylor on Facebook. Yes, God can even use Facebook. I have become close to several people this way. Some people I have yet to meet. The Lord drew John and I together as friends by praying for a mutual friend. We began to correspond. Then one day he called me in California to pray for me, all the way from Texas. When we talked his story began to unfold. He shared how he rededicated his life to the Lord years ago after feeling stuck in religion. John and his wife Connie had embarked on having a closer, more intimate relationship with Jesus Christ. He experienced the power of the Holy Spirit in his life and wanted more. He said when he was touched by the Holy Spirit, it was better than any drink or anything else the world had to offer. They started attending a church where the Holy Spirit was moving and working. They saw that miracles were not just an occurrence of the past and not just a Bible history lesson. He shared that he discovered how to soak in the presence of the Holy Spirit and this changed his life. John is a humble man who just wants the Lord to use him to help others like the Lord has helped him. He wants others to experience the love, forgiveness, salvation and healing touch that he received.

Just because a person attends a church or just believes does not mean they have a relationship with Jesus. A relationship with Jesus is our only assurance into Heaven. Not everyone will read the Bible. Sometimes the only Bible they will ever read will be through someone else's life. John's desire is that the Lord will make his life a Bible for others to read.

Certain people do not cross our path by accident or coincidence. Some people come into our life for a reason and sometimes just for a season. We need to look at our life through spiritual eyes to see our purpose and the purpose of others who have come into our life. Everyone has a story and if we are willing vessels it will bring God glory. God can re-write our story. John's story has and is bringing God glory by changing the lives of everyone he meets.

John has been anointed by God to bring healing to hurting people. He answered this call from Jesus with faith and obedience. Not only has his life changed, but the lives of countless others have also changed. You will see this as you read his testimony and the testimonies of others he has touched.

John was invited to appear on Christian television a few years ago. He was interviewed and shared the stories of miracles that follow his ministry.

If you are wanting to know if there is more to God than what you have experienced, read John's story of hope, help and healing of hurting people that only God can provide when He is sought with supernatural faith and all of your heart.

This book is about the miracles that follow John Taylor, the praying cowboy. It is about the big miracles and the small ones too. Miracles still happen today and God is still at work like he was 2,000 years ago. In Hebrews 13:8, the Bible says God is the same yesterday, today and always. In our busy and distracted lives we often miss the miracles that are happening every day; we have become blinded to them. Some of us limit God by our unbelief or put him in a box because religion has misrepresented Him by their manmade doctrines and legalism. Man and religion have restricted and have made a mockery of the works of the Holy Spirit. God answers our prayers in different ways according to the plans He has for us and knowing our future, therefore knowing what is best for us and what the final outcome will be.

Signs, wonders and miracles should follow us if we could only believe what the Bible says about God and if we abide in Him. Why is it so easy for people to believe in the supernatural in regards to

Introduction

the other things that are in this world, but doubt that God still works that way today? Miracles are more than just physical healing; they apply to every aspect of our lives if we are willing to put our faith out there. There is only one true God who can manifest these divine appointments in our lives. That would be the God of the Bible who sent Jesus to save us and restore us. When we have faith and say yes to following and obeying Him, we untie His hands to move on our behalf, whatever that situation may be. John Taylor is a loving and honest man who has a childlike faith. He is here to show us and tell us through his stories that God is still the God of miracles. People have traveled far to have John pray for them. John has also traveled far to pray for others. This is his heart and life.

His ministry, pictures of the horse and cross, CD's and DVD's have reached and touched people all over this country and beyond.

We need to awake from our doubt and unbelief and go after the life God has for us, a life that has meaning and eternal value. I encourage you if you are hurting in any way or if you want more than religion, to read John's testimonies of hope, signs, wonders and miracles. I have come to respect this man very much. He has rekindled a desire in me to go after all God has for me and to press past the limits I have put in my faith.

On New Year's Day of 2012, John was ordained into the ministry by his personal pastor, Ray McNames. The Lord spoke to Pastor Ray in the early hours of that morning, took him out of a deep sleep and asked him to do this for John. John Taylor has been the Lord's faithful servant by loving and praying for others. I believe this was God's way of honoring and rewarding him.

This book is the first one with more to follow. These stories come from just two of John's many journals on miracles.

May God speak to you as you read about the praying cowboy from Texas.

Robin White

Make My Life a Bible

Lyrics written by Cary Gilham and used with permission

"Lord, make my life a Bible, it is the only one some people will ever read. I want to walk so close to You that the blinded might see, and when they read through my pages they will see You and not me. Lord, I want to stay as far away from religion as I can, no longer bound by passing down tradition of man. It's neither here nor there, a millionaire or as poor as can be. Lord, make me a blessing to those around me. Lord, if people see any good in me it is all because of You. Be magnified, glorified in the things I say and do. And every day help me to stay the tower of light, because through the world walks the prisoner and you placed the keys in my life. Lord, when they read through my pages may they see You and not me."

Lord, I Want MY Life to be Like a Bible

In 2001, I was 62 years old. I had been a Christian for as long as I could remember, before my teenage years. In my twenties, I was out of church more than I was in it. I had been living the world's way for way too long. I had broken too many of the Lord's commandments. I knew Jesus had died for me, but I also knew I had not done one thing for Him.

One day an evangelist group came to a church in Honey Island, Texas. My life was about to radically change. Rick, his wife Debra, and their daughter Natasha, were part of this revival team. They were very talented people. Rick would preach and all three of them would sing. What stood out the most to me was the presence of the Holy Spirit around them. I also remember a lady named Beth who sang a song called, *I'll be back*. It was between the preaching and the song that I felt the Holy Spirit had touched me in a very special way.

A short time later Cary Gilham sang, *Make My Life a Bible*. This song has now become the most important song in my life. I listen to it almost every day. It is really a prayer, and I take that song with me when I pray for others.

Lord make my life a Bible, it is the only one that some people will ever read. When they read through the pages may they see You and not me. I rededicated my life to Jesus during that revival. I was not drawn back by religion, but by the power of the Holy Spirit.

The Holy Spirit in My Truck

In 2001, Connie and I had been attending a church for a short time. The Pastor's wife Judy was ill and in the hospital. One day as I was making a trip where one of my fillies was boarded, I got a strong impression in my spirit that I was supposed to go to Beaumont in Texas and pray for her. I had never prayed for anyone in my life! I thought to myself that this can't be right, but the impression just became stronger.

When I finally reached the barn and saw all the guys, I began to shoot the bull with them and forgot all about it. However, the Lord has a much better memory. If you think the Holy Spirit was dealing with me on that trip to the barn, you should have been in the truck with me on the way home! It felt like the Holy Spirit was sitting with me in the passenger's seat just waiting. I know now that He was.

Driving the twenty miles back to my house was quite an event. I was talking out loud, waving my arms and protesting, "This can't be right, not me! Y'all know me! Who am I to do this? Something is wrong!" I kept saying out loud, "I have never prayed for anyone so this must be a mistake!" I was talking to the Father, Son and Holy Spirit. I beat the dashboard with my fist and I was yelling, "I don't know who it is that You need to go pray for that woman! You need to go find him! It is not me!" While driving that last mile down the road to my home, I gave up and said I would go. I will go tomorrow, yes tomorrow. The presence of the Lord was overpowering when I got into the house. The Holy Spirit did not stay in the truck, right on in the house with me He came. Nothing like this had ever happened to me before, but I was going to go tomorrow and that was that. Two hours of "Gun Smoke" was about to come on television. I love Festus (Ken Curtis) and I was going to watch it. That was not going to happen either. I could not be still. I kept getting up and walking around. Finally, I gave up again. I took a shower and headed to Beaumont with the Holy Spirit with me all the way.

When I walked into the room there was a nurse fooling around with all of those machines. The pastor was not there. Sister Judy was not coherent. I thought I would just wait until the nurse completed her work and I would close the door and pray the best I could. The nurse closed the door and left. Did she not see me in there? They did not know me and there I was shut in that room with this lady. No way did they not see me. I am six foot six and two hundred and forty five pounds. Then I remembered the Lord can do anything and He worked it out that I wasn't seen so I would not be asked to leave.

I threw the big western hat in the chair and went over and put my hand on her forehead. Then I prayed the best prayer that I knew how. I was still feeling the powerful presence of God. His presence comes in the form of the Holy Spirit. I then went home.

Two hours later I called the hospital and the pastor was there. I told him my story and asked him how she was doing. He said she was sitting up, eating supper and watching television. He then asked if I wanted to talk to her and I quickly replied yes. She went home the next day, praise God!

Let me tell you the real shocker about the first person the Lord had me pray for...I say, "Let me" because now I consider it an honor and privilege to pray for any of God's children. Religion, race, color or creed is of no interest to me. It is all about Christ and His children, and that is what all of you are to me. Anyway, Judy informed me of something two or three weeks later. She said, "John, when you prayed for me I had left my body, I was going 'home'." My heart was in my throat and I could not catch my breath. Judy was dying the moment I began to pray. I know now why I was sent there with a sense of urgency. God's intervention was activated through prayer. I could only say, "My God, my God, why would You use someone like me?!"

It is important for me to say what I am about to say. There is no way that I think that I have healed anyone. Until this day, I have yet to heal my first person and I never will! There is only one God who can do something like that. After that prayer with Sister Judy, I was willing to leave it at that. I thought then it was a onetime thing, but it was not.

The pastor and Judy began taking me all over the place to pray for people. At the time I didn't really think I would enjoy this, but it didn't take long before I realized I did. I was walking away after praying for people with a whole new outlook on life. There is no sin that I have walked away from that will ever come close to the warmth and closeness I feel walking with the Lord. Nothing the world has to offer is as enjoyable as this. Being the country intellectual that I am, I can say it best like this: I literally was basking and wallowing in the presence of the Holy Spirit. That is why I always tell people, "Thank you for letting me pray for you!" It really was and is a pleasure to pray for God's people. There is a Bible verse that I base my whole ministry on. In Matthew 22: 37-40, "And He replied to him. You shall love the Lord your God with all your heart and with all your soul and with all your mind (intellect). This is the great (most important, principal) and first commandment. And a second like it, You shall love your neighbor as (you do) yourself. These two commandments sum up and upon them depend all the Law and the Prophets."

It cannot get any plainer than that. As time went on, I was living in glory on earth. I could not imagine the Lord using someone like me.

Brain Tumor

I began to pray with more and more people in their homes and at church. One Sunday morning a mother showed up at church. The pastor told me that she was coming to the altar and wanted me to pray for her five year old daughter Karlie. She had a brain tumor. The tumor was growing and causing Karlie to have unbearable headaches. To make matters worse, the doctors could not operate because the tumor was in her line of vision. As soon as I heard this Karlie and her mother came through the church doors. Her mother was encouraging her to come towards me while guiding her with her hand on the small of her back. Both of them were looking at me with great expectation. I have no words to describe how I felt. The inside of me turned into jelly and I would have liked to have been somewhere else. I knew I was nothing and that "John" didn't have any power. I was a total wreck and I bowed my head and prayed. I prayed, "Lord God, You know I am nothing and I can do nothing. Lord, give me strength and help me. Please answer my prayers for this little girl! I will do anything Lord, anything!" I like to have as many people who are willing to join me when I lay hands on someone to pray. I believe there is more power in prayer this way. It says in the Bible wherever two or more are gathered in His name, He is in our midst. That does not mean He is not with us when we pray by ourselves, it is just saying there is always power in numbers.

I had started anointing people with oil when I prayed for them. Anointing oil is symbolic to the Holy Spirit and expresses our faith in His power. I touched the tip of my oiled finger to Karlie's forehead and we agreed in prayer. We felt the presence of the Holy Spirit in a mighty way.

Later I was told that the tumor was still there but had stopped growing. The headaches had gone away and Karlie was back to living like a normal child. The Lord spared her vision and her life. I gave all the praise to God. It is so important to give God thanks when He moves on our behalf. It is too easy to take it for granted. It pleases His heart, just like yours is pleased when your kids thank you after you do something for them.

One summer my friend Perry suggested I start keeping a journal of everything that God was doing in my life. Many people were prayed for from February to June that year, so many that I can't remember them all. I was not aware that God was sending as many people as He was. In 2006, I was starting my third journal of all the miracles and many answered prayers.

What a privilege, honor and blessing that God is using me! I am someone who does not feel worthy of this. Again, it is not me, but God working through me and I give Him all the glory. I am just a willing vessel.

Breast Cancer

This testimony is one of my favorites. This happened just before I started keeping journals of what God was doing, but I remember it so well.

I got a call from my friend Beth who asked if I would meet her friend Lori. She had been diagnosed with breast cancer. The doctors in Beaumont said they could not help her and decided to send her to Galveston Hospital.

I drove forty five miles to meet Lori in a market parking lot. This was the first time I had ever seen her. Lori got in my pickup truck and we parked next to a trash dumpster to pray (the Lord will meet you anywhere). I shared some of my testimony with her and wanted to build her faith, not in me, but in the Word of God; faith that Jesus with the power of the Holy Spirit could heal her.

I anointed Lori with oil and we prayed. The presence of the Holy Spirit was overpowering. The next day Lori went to Galveston Hospital as the doctors suggested. She was informed that day that there was no sign of cancer and they told her to go home. I am sure this baffled the doctors. She ran up and down the hospital halls yelling, "Praise God!"

Trip to Heaven's gate

So many blessings came to me as a result of praying for the Lord's people. The presence of the Holy Spirit was with all of us. However, I knew I was not quite where I needed to be with the Lord. A short while later another miracle occurred. This time the miracle was for me. It was December 16, 2002 when I awakened suddenly. It was three AM. I was wide awake and noticed a glow at the foot of my bed. I realized it was an angel. I was not dreaming. I was not alarmed in the least. I then heard these words, "John, it's time to go home." I answered simply with, "Okay!" I was not afraid, I felt at peace. In an instant I felt myself going straight up. No space shuttle could match that speed. In a fleeting second, I could see the earth below my feet getting smaller and smaller. The angel was on my right and holding my arm. I know now that was my guardian angel. We were moving so fast and then suddenly stopped. I saw a beautiful white wall of clouds in front of me. I could not see over, under or around them and without a doubt, I knew Heaven's gate was on the other side of it. There were still so many people depending on me on earth, including hundreds of people I had yet to meet. There was that one thing in my life that I did not want to meet Jesus with, but I would have been allowed to enter despite my imperfection. My angel then said, "John, you can go in or you can go back." I answered with, "I better go back." My spirit wanted to stay because I have never felt that kind of peace before. Words cannot describe what I saw and felt. Next thing I knew, I was back in my bed. Some people will think that this was just a dream, but it wasn't. My confirmation to this truth was that the Holy Spirit stayed with me for three days and nights after that. I felt like Moses after being in God's presence. I was walking in Heaven on earth.

The next morning I made sure every area of my life was covered by the blood of Jesus. I repented of what I needed to and made sure everything was right between me and my Lord. There was one corner in my life that needed sweeping out. By the time the sun had risen in the Eastern sky, I had prayed and let it go. There is no sin worth hanging on to and after I released it, my corner was swept clean and I have never felt so loved in all of my life. I was ready to go but willing to stay.

A Child's Boil

Then my job as a prayer warrior that God gave me really began to pick up pace. The Lord was sending more and more people to me who needed prayer or a miracle. One day as I was leaving the grocery store, a friend of mine named Jennifer saw me. She yelled from across the lot, "John! You are just the person I wanted to see. Would you pray for my little boy?" She had heard about the miracles God was doing through my ministry. She was holding an infant in her arms. I looked at her and said, "What do you think, Jennifer?" She showed me a nasty boil he had on his skin. Right there in the middle of the parking lot we had a prayer meeting. We did not care who was looking at us. We went to the Lord with faith in prayer.

I heard a few days later that the Lord had healed him as well. The boil disappeared. I noticed I was starting to pray in a lot of different places. I did not care; I was willing to pray anywhere. I never asked anyone if I could pray for them, they would ask me. By them asking for prayer, they were exercising their faith. Without faith, it is impossible to please God (Hebrews 11:6).

I was praying everywhere, on the road, the courthouse, Wal-Mart, just to name a few.

Jaw Pain

One morning Connie was getting ready for work and asked me, "Do you have anyone to pray for today?" "No," I quickly replied. "All I am going to do today is buy license plates." That is what I thought anyway. I had not factored in God's plan for me that day.

I was purchasing them from a beautiful young lady named Sherrie. It was obvious that she had a problem with her jaw. She said when she began to eat or sing; she experienced tremendous pain in her jaw. The doctors told her they did not know what to do to help her condition. She asked if I would be willing to pray for her. I told her to call me sometime and we could meet after work or while she was on her lunch break. She then said, "I have been on my lunch break for five minutes now." I told her to meet me outside of the courthouse and she showed me which door she would be using to exit. I got in my van and drove closer to the building noticing that there weren't any parking spaces. It must have been a busy court day because I had parked a block away. As I walked past the door, the door that she said she would come out of, a car left the parking space in front of the door. I returned with my van just as she was walking out. Sherrie and I both knew without a doubt, the Lord had opened up that parking space. The Holy Spirit had once again showed up. I anointed her with oil and prayed. I felt God's presence so strong that I thought we were floating off the ground. She felt the power of God just as strong as I did.

I got a call three months later from Sherrie, she informed me that the Lord had healed her. We prayed again, this time giving thanks, praise and the glory of it to God.

The Muslim and My Cancer

I thought maybe I was just getting old. When working around my horse barn I seemed to be resting in my lawn chair more often. I would pet the cat my granddaughter Kristen gave me because I was home alone and she didn't want me to be lonely. In October, I finally went to the doctor. The first time I met him was four years prior and we became friends despite the fact that he was a Muslim and I was a Christian. After that initial, lengthy first meeting, he had said the prophets were dead and there were no more miracles. He said it was all science now. I told him we would have to agree to disagree because I had seen many miracles happen. This doctor is not one of them Muslim radicals. He is a good, kind and caring man. Our conversation was not tense or hostile in the slightest. I love this man and told him so.

Now four years later I am in his office having our usual friendly visit. After a short time he asked what I was there for that day. I said, "Doc, I have cancer." He took a full step backwards and said, "You don't have cancer! Where do you think you have cancer?" I told him it was in my lungs, lymph nodes, or somewhere in my chest area. Again he said, "Who told you that you have cancer?" I replied by telling him the Holy Spirit had told me. He then checked my lymph nodes and said they were clear but added, "John, because you are a friend of mine and because you pray for people, I am going to send you to have a chest X-ray." I knew in my heart that he loved me. I went and had my X-ray that same day. That was on a Monday. Friday morning at 8:15 AM his nurse Kathy called me and said, "John, you have a mass in your chest." She was very concerned. Kathy and I were friends also and had prayed together for other things. I answered with, "I know." She then informed me that she had scheduled a Cat Scan for the following Tuesday. I wasn't alarmed. You see, I still was ready to go but willing to stay. I hung up the phone and went into my office. I have an office now since the kids left home. I sat in my desk chair and began to pray. I felt something happening. The feeling started dead center in my chest and was intensifying. I started to enjoy it and quit praying. Nothing, and I mean nothing, can take the place of that feeling. I felt the healing touch and the presence of the Holy Spirit.

When the Cat Scan came back, it was completely clear! Yes! I gave all the praise to God. I got up and walked out to the horse barn. Just by walking I knew I had been healed. I felt stronger and was breathing better. I didn't need anything else to convince me. The doctor still wanted me to have a bone density test the following week. I walked in his office just to sign in at the window and then go across the hall for the test. I saw Kathy behind the window looking for something. I never see her up front; she is always in the back with patients. I know the Lord had her up front. I called her name through the little hole in the glass and said, "Tell doc when I have that bone density test it will be clear." She replied, "Okay John," but I could tell she was distracted. I repeated what I had said to her a second time. I had her attention then. She said, "Okay John, I will," and she did, and the test was clear. No sign of cancer, mass was gone as well. Then the Lord told me to testify (share my story).

Rocks, Oil and Healing

Six months ago I had sold a piece of property in Buna, Texas to a young couple with children. I had promised to give them a load of rocks for their driveway. Now it was six months later and I had not kept my word. It was Wednesday morning and I said to myself that I was going to go get that burden off my back today. I thought this was my idea, but it wasn't. I called and scheduled a rock truck to meet me at the Dairy Queen in Buna later that day. We met and the truck followed me over to the property. The truck dumped the rocks and then left. Then out of the house came a couple, they were older than me. I was sixty five at that time. They were nice people and we began to talk. I heard the Holy Spirit three times prompting me to tell them about my cancerous mass the Lord had healed. I decided that I better do it because it was more than a suggestion. I proceeded to tell them the whole story about my mass. When I finished, the lady stepped back. I thought to myself oh no, we have an unbeliever. I was wrong. Then she said, "Do you see that lawn chair in front of your truck?" I told her yes. I saw a chair in front of my truck at the edge of a beautiful vegetable garden. She said that was as far as she could walk, then she would have to rest for fifteen minutes so she would have enough strength to go back to the house. Sometimes her husband wants her to look at something in the garden. Guess what? Forty five minutes before this conversation began; this lady's doctor called her and told her she had a mass in her chest.

This was another set up by the Lord. The rocks I delivered today were actually on time, the Lord's time. God's presence (Holy Spirit) had already fallen as I completed my testimony. She then asked if I would pray for her. "Absolutely," I said. That is when I remembered the anointing oil I had purchased weeks ago. At the time I thought it was an impulsive buy, now I knew it was not. You can't buy a miracle or purchase God's presence in a bottle. The oil is prayed over in faith and is symbolic to the Holy Spirit. It is a symbol used often in healing; acknowledging and reminding us that there is power in God's Spirit when combined with our faith. The Bible says that if we have faith but not works (action showing we have faith), then our faith is dead. People can be healed by God without oil. God can move in any way and anytime He wants to. It is in act of faith. Not ordinary faith, but supernatural faith that believes what we pray for will be manifested by the power of His Spirit and in the name of Jesus Who died for our infirmities.

I told her I had the anointing oil in my truck. She quickly replied with a yes, she had faith. The Spirit was strong when we prayed and tears were running down my cheeks. It was beautiful!

It was one week to the day as I was driving my one ton truck on the freeway, that I received a call on my cell phone from this lady. "John, I wanted to call and let you know that the Lord healed me." I pulled the truck off the road and into the grass. I felt the Holy Spirit on me again and I could not see. I said to her on the phone, "Praise God, He is the one!" "Yes, but you prayed for me." And that is all I did. I prayed, God did the rest. She agreed that God did the work and she just wanted to thank me. She went on to say that she was visiting relatives she hadn't seen in years and was now able to mow the lawn. She was praising God all over Buna, Texas. She jokingly shared how she had visited the new Wal-Mart and her husband wanted to know why she wasn't getting tired because he was.

It was about three months later when she called and asked if I would drive to Jasper to pray for her brother who had terrible headaches. We went and prayed and once again, the Lord granted our request. He doesn't have headaches anymore. I stand here in awe, now and forever will I praise God.

In 2006, I went to a farm and ranch to buy a gate. The owners Sam and Linda told me about a lady customer who had recently visited their store. On the wall she saw a painting of Warrior, my stallion. As she looked she saw that my name was on the painting. She looked at Sam and Linda and said, "John Taylor, do you know what he did? He went to Buna to pray for a friend of mine with a heart problem. She has not had that problem since then!" When I heard that I thought, thank you Jesus! I wish I knew who that lady was. I would love to talk to her. Keep sending them Lord, keep sending them. I hope and pray that Jesus is pleased with me.

How Prayers are Answered

What a blessing when you are out somewhere and people see you and ask for prayer. This is the way my life is now and how great my life has become. I will pray anywhere and anytime. This is God's calling on my life. I have prayed in the post office as people waited patiently in line. I prayed in another city for a lady named Joann and her son. He had a heart problem and she needed a better job. Both prayers were answered. He wants to bless us and bring healing into our lives, but more importantly He wants us to know the "Healer." We can only do this by surrendering our life to Christ, every aspect of it. We have to talk to Him through prayer, and listen and watch for His answers. He will speak to our spirit. I am not talking about an audible voice, but an inner voice. When we accept Christ as Lord over our life, the Holy Spirit then resides in us. Most of us don't take the time to get to know Him. We pray quick popcorn prayers of petitions and go on our way. We get to know His character and who He is by reading the Bible, His living and active words to us. It is not a history book, but God's voice revealing His promises, plans, wisdom, warnings and love for us. He wants a relationship with us, not a ritualistic practice of religion. Religion won't save you. It was the religious people who nailed Jesus to the cross.

As you seek Him through His Word with sincerity, you will notice that there will be times when words "fly" off the page at you. That is the main way He communicates with us. There are promises in His Word for us that do not happen automatically, but when we put faith and our voice in praying His promises, we can be assured that He hears us and will answer us.

God will not be mocked. If we are using Him like a Santa Claus just when we want something, our prayers will be hindered. Living in intentional disobedience to His ways will also hinder, as well as unforgiveness towards others and unrepentant sin. We all sin every day and as long as we are human there will be a battle between our flesh and spirit.

Repenting is changing our mind and our ways to living a lifestyle that is pleasing to Him. All we need to do is confess when we have messed up and He is quick and faithful to forgive us. The key is to surrender and seek Him with all of our heart, and to put Him first in our lives above everything else. We need to go back to our "first love," Jesus. He wants to love us back and rain down His goodness in our lives. "Seek ye first the kingdom of God and all of His righteousness, and everything else shall be added unto you." Matthew 6:33. Like human relationships, it takes two parties to speak and listen. His commands are not to restrict us, but to close the door to sin so blessings can flow to and through us. We tie His hands when we live in rebellion as our flesh dictates. The choice is ours to make. We will never be perfect. We need to let Him work in us as an ongoing process of molding our character so it attracts others to Him.

We all have our issues or "thorns" we struggle with. We can't accomplish these goals in our strength; it has to be by His strength and power working in us. It is His grace that empowers us to do what we can't on our own. This is where true freedom lies as opposed to the bondage and consequences of intentional sin. Grace is never a license to sin. As appealing as sin is, as honey to a bee, it will end up "stinging" you in one way or another. That is the deception of it, because it appears to be the way of happiness and it is the world's way. It will bite you in the end and can be deadly.

There are two kingdoms, God's kingdom and Satan's kingdom. "The thief comes only in order to steal and kill and destroy. I came that they may have and enjoy life, and have it in abundance. (to the full, till it overflows)." John 10:10. Abraham was blessed abundantly and beyond measure because of his love and obedience to God. We are heirs to Abraham if we live our lives by putting God first in everything; therefore we are promised the same blessings that he received. "And He will do exceedingly, abundantly, beyond all we can ask or think according to the riches that are in Christ Jesus." Ephesians 3:20

Catholic Radio Miracles

June 22, 2005 was a landmark day in my life. Tommy Mclain invited me to go live on the air on his radio program. "Moving To Heaven" was the name of the program. I had told his staff that I, "Have prayer, will travel." They liked that. This was a Catholic radio station. When I walked into the lobby of the radio station there were about twelve people there, ten Catholics and two Baptists. They all wanted me to pray for them and I was honored beyond compare. We were there to pray for the radio audience, but as it turned out they needed prayer the most that day. I formed what I call a "posse" and we all laid hands on each other for prayer. There is power in numbers, just like the Bible says. I do that as much as possible.

Since that day I have heard confirmation that three of those people received answered prayer. Surgery was canceled for one of them that following week. There was someone else who had asked for prayer that day and he was a Franciscan priest, fifty years in the ministry. I was taken aback by that request, but I did as the Lord led me. I may be a cowboy, but I am not a stupid man. I always make sure people pray and lift me up before I pray for others. I had asked Father Duane to pray for me that day and he did. The Lord did a healing on that priest. He did a healing on the three people I had heard from. It is possible there were more that I just didn't hear about.

God set me up for that divine appointment and it was one of the greatest days of my life. I was on the radio with them once a week and the Holy Spirit always showed up. Radio Maria prays for me and supports my ministry. Tommy and his then fiancé Carolyn became wonderful friends of mine. I can never have too many friends. Because of the radio program I began to get many calls for prayer. A woman named Josephine was one of the first to call me. I didn't realize there were a lot of black Catholics. Not that it matters or is important, I just didn't know. Looking back on the prayers Josephine and I shared, I can feel the presence of Jesus. We prayed for her daughter in law, Kim. She was in the middle of her pregnancy and having serious problems with it. To make matters worse, her husband Cory did not have a job. Things were stressful to say the least. Josephine and I met in the parking lot of Central Mall in Port Arthur, Texas. That was the first of many prayers to follow for her family. She heard me on Radio Maria. She had only heard half of a prayer on the air and felt led to call me regarding her concerns. The problems with Kim's pregnancy ceased and the baby was born several months later, normal and healthy. Within a month of that, her husband found a job. The Lord gave him favor and he passed all the tests pertaining to the job, and the job came with benefits. Only God Himself can do all of these things. Josephine and I were quick to go back to prayer to thank God and give Him praise. He gets all the credit.

The Healing Inside the Womb

To me, the most beautiful miracles are when God heals little children. My daughter-in-law's cousin told a lady named Danielle about my ministry. I came home one evening around eight and Danielle called. Danielle was pregnant and had an ultra sound earlier that day. The tests showed that the baby's arms and legs were abnormally short. The baby had major deformities and the doctors were concerned. They were going to take the baby by C-section the following day. Needless to say, Danielle was beside herself. However, Jesus is alive and is still on the throne. I wasn't the only one praying for her. I prayed for her on the phone and the presence of God was strong. It turned out that the C-section that was planned for the following day was not going to happen. The Lord intervened and did so quickly. Danielle had called at eight PM and she was in labor by nine PM and in the hospital. Baby Dustin met the world that night with normal sized arms and legs. I did not hear about it until the next morning. These folks did not know me, nor did I know them. I had to see that baby and I wanted to hold him. When I entered her room her husband was there and one set of grandparents. More importantly, Dustin was in the room and I got to hold that miracle. I never fail to give God thanks for answered prayers. Since that day, I have been in Danielle's home on several occasions and prayed for one thing or another. The Holy Spirit was with me every time.

The Healing Inside the Womb

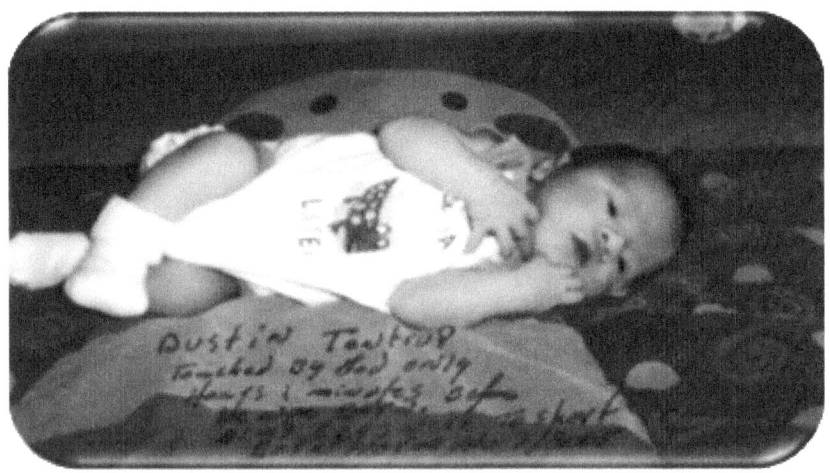

Wording on photo: DustinTentrup, touched by God only hours & minutes before he was born. Arms and legs were too short. Born normal. 7/2005

It can Happen to You too

There have been many prayers for many people and I wish I could remember them all. Some of these stories are from memory. I regret not keeping a journal prior to 2005. If it were not for my friend Perry, I would have never started writing what God has done in my life and these stories. I have said it before, but it is important for me to reiterate again, what is happening in my life can happen in your life too. You can grow in His grace and receive more of the Holy Spirit as you walk out your life with the Lord. It can be in your personal life or in your ministry.

Everyone has different gifts that were given to them when they were created. God deposited the gifts He wanted us to have in each of us. They are unwrapped gifts until we do our part. Our part is to seek Him so He can show us what we have locked up on the inside of us. Most of us have no idea what potential we have. We were all destined for great things. He gives each of us different gifts for us to use to serve Him, bless others and ourselves in the process. There are so many other gifts besides the gift of supernatural faith. It will make your life satisfying and give it eternal value.

There is nothing in my past that compares to my life now with the Lord in it. I never look back and think about my old life and sinful past. I do look back on what God has done in my life and tell Him thank You for the blessings, let me have more.

Lord, as they read through my pages may they see You and not me. As you read through my pages remember this, if I wasn't telling you the truth, the Holy Spirit would have left me and my ministry a long time ago. I have prayed that as you read through the pages in this book, that you would feel the Holy Spirit. I pray that Jesus reveals Himself to you in a personal way. The miracles that the Lord has blessed me to witness have only just begun with what you have read so far.

Also, I want whoever reads this to know that there is no way I would meet Jesus after lying in His name. Even though I have not taken a dime for praying for someone, there have been times when people have stuffed hundred dollar bills in my pocket. Sometimes I have to drive a long way to pray for people. I will not even take the price of fuel for my automobile. When I meet Jesus I want Him to be pleased with me. Telling lies in Jesus' name would cost me for eternity. This cowboy does not know how long eternity is, but I know it is way pass suppertime.

The Wound that only He can Heal

Within that same year a woman named Nina called regarding her 59 year old son. He had an open wound between his shoulder blades that just would not heal. He suffered with this for quite a while. They heard about my ministry through TommyThomas's radio program "Moving To Heaven." Tommy insisted I call in and pray for his listeners along with the Radio Maria group. The group prayed with Nina as well. Nina and I prayed on the phone and the anointing showed up. Amazingly, Nina called me three days later and informed me that the wound was closing.

Even now at this stage of my prayer warrior ministry the Lord has given me, I am still amazed. He gave me the gift of supernatural faith and anointed my hands with His healing power. However, I am becoming less and less surprised.

He is Jehovah Rapha, which means God is our healer. We can call on Him at any time. We do not need to feel "worthy" first. He has grace and mercy and knows we are all human. We don't have to try to get our act straight first before we give Him reign of our life. We approach Him first and ask Him to help us. He then starts a process of transforming us into what He has called us to be. It is only by the empowerment of His grace that we change deep seeded behavior. That is why He sent His Son Jesus to the cross; to forgive us and set us free. He did give man a free will. It has to be our choice to accept this free gift.

It is not the "good" people who enter into Heaven. It is the people who have made Him their Lord and have an ongoing relationship with Him. He knows our suffering. He experienced suffering Himself in a way that we can never imagine or comprehend. He was tempted, rejected, lonely, scared, betrayed and then beat beyond human recognition. His flesh was ripped from His body by "religious" people who could not discern or believe What and Who was standing right in front of them. He knew this was going to happen, but He agreed to it anyway, for you and for me. He bore all of our sins on that cross so we did not have to. Yet to this day, He is still mocked and scoffed at by people who are deceived and have hardened their hearts. They have found other "gods" or idols (people or things) to worship. We can even worship ourselves and put "I" on the throne.

There is only ONE God and He sent His Son Jesus to save us from judgment if we let Him. He left His Holy Spirit (His presence) with us on earth until He returns. He does not send people to hell (hell is just as real as Heaven). WE send ourselves there when we reject Him and His outstretched arms towards us.

God is love and He loves you. He was forsaken, but He will never forsake you. His love is everlasting. It does not matter what you have done or where you have been. Jesus died so you could be forgiven and with Him in Heaven. The choice is up to you.

Healed From Drugs

Trudy heard of my healing ministry. Trudy had a progressive drug problem and was constantly having run-ins with the law. She asked if I would pray for her. She told me her story of addiction. Her mother was with her and I asked her if she would join me in prayer. Her mother and I prayed for her. I could tell that Trudy was sincere in wanting help. She was at the end of her rope and wanted Jesus to help her. The anointing filled the whole room as we prayed. Three times during that prayer I asked the Lord to make Trudy sick if she did drugs again. You better be careful what you pray for. Several weeks later I got a phone call. Every time she slipped up and caved in to doing drugs she became very ill. Trudy checked herself into a drug rehabilitation center. She's free from drugs due to the power, mercy and grace of God.

The Bulldozer and Cancer

The Lord can even use a bulldozer. The Lord can arrange and make things happen by using any method He chooses. That was the case when I met Les. I needed a bulldozer. Before Les and I started talking business, I began to testify (share) what God had done in my life and about my ministry. "You know," he said, "My daughter Pam has cancer. Maybe I can bring her to your house for prayer?" I told him absolutely, the sooner the better. Within a short time Les showed up with Pam and his wife Laura. Pam had cancer in her female organs and was scheduled for surgery the following week. We prayed the prayer of faith and agreement. By the time Pam went in for surgery, all the cancer was gone. This was a complete miracle.

The Lord desires for us to be healed mentally and emotionally as well. "Faith is the substance of all things hoped for, the evidence of things not seen." Hebrews 11:1 NKJV.

Faith is what moves the Hand of God, not our need. Faith in His Son Jesus and the power of the Holy Spirit. It is not complicated, we just make it complicated.

Yes, there are times when not everyone receives immediate physical healing. There are several different reasons for this which will be discussed more in detail later. He is no respecter of persons. He loves us all the same. No one is more worthy to receive than someone else.

The Power of Praise

The Lord inhabits the praises of His people. It invites his presence. That is why there is power in worship; it is one of our spiritual weapons. It should not be just a routine to sing three songs and hurry up and get to the message. People can feel the Holy Spirit during sincere times of worship. You can invite His presence in your home or car just by worshiping.

It's always important to thank Him and give Him praise. A grateful heart increases what He is able to do on our behalf. All good things that come to us ultimately come through Him. Satan hates it when we praise, because he cannot stay in an atmosphere of praise. He wants to be worshiped, too.

The Word of God is a spiritual weapon. When we speak and pray the Word of God (scripture), the devil has to flee. When we call on and pray in the name of Jesus, the devil has to flee. Giving Him thanks and praise is giving credit where credit is due, so we don't take our eyes off of Him and put them on man. He does use people as vessels, if they are willing to aid Him in answering the prayers of others.

The Lord can Work in a Funny Way

The Lord also has a sense of humor. Les's wife Laura took me to the side and said, "John, Les needs prayer too, but he won't let you pray for him." I responded with, "Why would he say that, Laura? He is the one who set this prayer meeting up for Pam." She told me that Les thought that I had so much power and he wanted it all to go to his daughter. I smiled and explained to her that I don't have any power. None, zip, however, we have unlimited power at our disposal. I am just a willing vessel. God does it all.

Speaking of humor, instead of Pam having surgery for cancer, she ended up having a pregnancy and a baby girl! Only God can change things so dramatically. Remember, her cancer was in her female organs.

Matthew 19:26, "And Jesus looked at them and said, with men this is impossible, but with God all things are possible." Time went on and Les called one morning and finally said, "John, what would a man have to do to get some of that anointing oil?" "Well Les, all he would have to do is ask for it. Who needs it, Les?" "I do!" He quickly replied, "I had foot surgery and they sent me home. I had to go back because I cannot pee!" I laughed to myself and told him with a smile on my face that I would be there within the hour. I went to the hospital and prayed for him and the problem was fixed. He was home in two hours.

Yes, the Lord is interested in all of our problems. Everything that concerns us concerns Him.

You And I Need Prayer

Like I said, I need prayer too. I sat down one day and prayed for myself. I was having problems getting motivated. I could not seem to get anything done and my energy level was low. I am always drained after I pray for people. This is not a complaint, just a fact. It will not stop me from praying for people though. I was having trouble putting one foot in front of another and getting things done. I took it to prayer and He was faithful to answer. Take that devil! Connie had pulled some muscles in her back. We took it to prayer and five seconds later it was gone. It is all about faith!

One time on a Sunday morning the pastor gave an altar call. Now I always take my journal to the altar, does not matter what church I am in. The journal has all the people I have prayed for in it. The Lord put it on my heart to take it to the altar every Sunday. When I bent my knees down at the altar, I got a terrible cramp in my right leg and this one was bad. I rarely get them in my right leg. Satan was trying to keep me from praying for God's people. I prayed and asked the Lord to remove this cramp in the name of Jesus so I could get on with His work. There is much power in calling on the name of Jesus; it is the Name above every other name. I then felt an instant and total relief. I always have a hard time getting rid of leg cramps, but not this time.

There is also power in pleading the blood of Jesus over a situation. It was the shed blood of Jesus on the cross that defeated Satan.

Once He knew He had defeated Satan, He closed his eyes and committed His Spirit to God. His work was finished. He finished it on the cross and threw us the keys to His Kingdom. The Lord does not love me more than anyone else. I was just obedient to do what He wanted me to do. He anointed me for this. He anoints different people with different gifts. We access them and His power by asking Him what He wants us to do, and then take a step of faith.

The anointing is the Holy Spirit's involvement (God's presence) in someone for a specific task. I believe He uses me because my heart goes after Him with a passion, and that is all He needs to be used by Him.

Like I said, we are not all called to have a healing ministry, but we are all called with the gifts we do have to serve Him. You don't have to have a ministry to pray and believe for healing for someone. I have just been anointed by Him to be used this way. The anointing is His ability on our ability; His Spirit working through us. I started off by just wanting to sing praises to the Lord, never mind the fact that I can't carry a tune. That does not matter, He looks at the heart. Praying for people was the last thing in the world I ever thought I would be doing. I did not choose this for myself. He chose me. Without His presence and anointing, I would have never witnessed the miracles I have witnessed, the ones you are reading about. There is so much satisfaction in what I do, helping others but also being able to be in is His presence so much. There isn't anything to describe what it is like to feel the Lord's presence. When you experience it, you will know and not doubt it. I will continue on with my assignment for as long as He allows.

I only want to do two things: share what God has done for me and pray for more people. I encourage you to pray as well. Little prayer, little power. Lots of prayer, a lot of power.

The Miracle of the Oil

This day will always be one of the greatest days of my life, compared only to the trip to Heaven's gate with my guardian angel. As I said before, the anointing is the involvement of the Holy Spirit. This can be on a person, a task or an atmosphere

The anointing oil is prayed over and used with faith for healing. It is symbolic and biblical, but not required for healing. It is an expression and an act of faith in the power of the Holy Spirit. It is like bowing our knees in prayer, an expression of humbling ourselves before God and acknowledging that we need His divine intervention. Exodus 30:31, "And say to the Israelites this is holy anointing oil (symbol of the Holy Spirit), sacred to Me alone throughout your generations."

Terry, a well to do business man came to visit me and we had some things to talk about. Terry is a contractor and we were discussing a job. When we were through talking business, Terry asked me to pray with him for his only child. We were sitting in his truck and it was getting dark. We had prayer together and I went into the house. When I came in through the kitchen door my wife was standing right behind me. Connie had been nagging me, something she normally never does. The oil in my bottle was getting low and she was concerned. I went to the back bedroom and started unloading my pockets. First my wallet, then my checkbook, etc. Connie was standing right next to me and I know now this was designed by

God. The Lord wanted her there as a witness. Then something happened. The last thing I took out of my pocket was the little bottle of anointing oil. Connie did not say a word. I set the bottle on the dresser and turned to her, and actually put my finger in front of her face. Before I could say a word she said, "You bought some more oil." Without a reply, I looked back and the bottle was full right up to the little black cap. I grabbed the bottle with both hands clutching it tightly. I said, "No, I did not." The tears started flowing down my cheeks and I have never felt the Holy Spirit as strong as I did that moment. "Then where did it come from?" She wanted to know. I knew and I told her, "There is no one living in this house but you and I, the Lord multiplied it."

Connie said, "Why would He do that?" I told her it was because I had been foolish and she then asked what I had done. I responded by telling her, "Connie, I have been thinking about quitting my prayer ministry." She wanted to know why I would even consider that. "Because of back stabbing, cut throating and the undermining of other people. It is like I know who is doing it and what they are saying." I then told her I would never again consider quitting unless the Lord wants me to.

Still clutching the bottle tightly with both of my hands, I was thinking how could I be so stupid to even consider quitting. Even during the time I was contemplating it, the Lord was still sending people who needed prayer right to my front yard. Connie said, "John, you can't tell anyone about this! If I did not live with you and see all of these things for myself, I would not believe it either." I told her no and that I was going to testify and share the power of the Lord. He is telling me, there is your oil boy, keep on going!

As time goes by there are many who do not believe, but there are also many who do have faith and believe in the power of the Lord, and He has healed them. I do not tell lies using the name of Jesus. There are some who have received Christ as they were being healed. If I had stopped, some people would not have been healed and others would not have been in an environment to receive Christ as their Savior. Lord, make my life a Bible, one drop at a time.

Miracles still happen, but Satan and doctrines of religion have stopped us from believing in supernatural events. They have been

The Miracle of the Oil

successful in convincing us that those type of incidents only happened in the "Bible days" and have since ceased to exist. We don't often experience them because of this belief. We often overlook them when they do happen. Like when you know you do not have enough money to pay the bills next month, but when that time comes around the money is in your account. Jesus multiplied fish and bread to feed thousands of people. He can multiply anything. And He said to them, "Cast the net on the right side of the boat and you will find [some]. So they cast the net and now they were not able to haul it in for such a big catch (mass, quantity) of fish [was in it]." John 21:6

Have you ever searched for something and could not find it, and then when you prayed it all of a sudden showed up? He suffered persecution, and He said we His people would be persecuted and ridiculed also. John 15:19, "If you belonged to the world, the world would treat you with affection and would love you as its own. But because you are not of the world {no longer one with it}, but I have chosen (selected) you out of the world; the world hates (detests) you. Remember that I told you, a servant is not greater than his master {is not superior to Him}. If they persecuted Me, they will also persecute you; if they kept My word and obeyed My teachings, they will also obey and keep yours. But they will do all of this to you {inflict all of this suffering on you} because of {your bearing} My name and on My account, they do not understand or know the One Who sent me." Hebrews 2:4, "[besides this evidence] it was also established and plainly endorsed by God. Who showed His approval of it by signs and wonders and various miraculous manifestations of [His] power and by imparting the gifts of the Holy Spirit [to the believers] according to His own will."

Anointing Oil and Hurricane Money

My friend Perry felt led by the Lord to play the harmonica. He felt inadequate in his ability and he politely told the Lord he could not do that. The Holy Spirit spoke to his spirit and told him that He would help him learn. In my opinion, Perry has become one of the best harmonica players in such a short period of time. He has suitcases full of all the different kind of harmonicas. Perry wanted to know if I would come to his church and speak. I felt honored by his request. I had not spoken to a congregation in this manner before. I told him I was not a preacher and all I do is testify and share what the Lord has done. He told me that was fine. Instantly I knew what I would say at his church. The Lord wanted me to share in the same way that I am sharing with you in this book.

My friend Cary was on tour along the East Coast, serving God with his music, ministry and comedy. One night he called me and said he heard that I was going to speak at Perry's church, and wanted to know if I could put it off until he could be there. Cary Gilham is his name, he wrote and sang the song, *Make My Life a Bible*. I told him I would ask the pastor and inquire about changing the date. I said, "However, if I do that, you will have to sing my song when I finish speaking." Cary agreed and I set it up with the pastor. During the time leading up to that date I prayed, "Lord, you know that I

Anointing Oil and Hurricane Money

am no one, without the power of the Holy Spirit this will be a flop. Lord, this is for Your glory to show Your power, help me to help You." I continued to pray along these lines right up to the hour that I was to speak.

One day I was driving my truck down highway 96. New Orleans had been totally destroyed by a hurricane. While I was riding along the Lord said, "You are going to get money when you speak at that church." I answered Him back by letting Him know that I don't take any money. He repeated it again and so did I. It was repeated for a third time. This time He said, "You are going to get two hundred dollars." And I still said, "I don't take money." The Holy Spirit was totally ignoring me. You can hear God's voice in your spirit, it can come as a strong thought or impression, but you will know when it is Him speaking. If you have developed a relationship with Him you will recognize His voice. He went on to say, "And this is what you are going to do with it. There are three hundred evacuees in Kountze, Texas. A large percentage of them are staying at the First Baptist Church in the city. You are to give the Hankramer Community Church back one hundred dollars, and the other hundred to Tony at the First Baptist Church for all the people they have staying there." I have had people shove twenty dollar bills in my pocket, even hundreds, but I have never taken a penny. I have no interest in financial gain in doing the Lord's work. Like I said, I have refused to take even gas money. The Lord has always provided for me, always! I felt then and I feel now that I should not take money for praying and testifying to people. I still believe the Lord will always provide for me like He always has. I receive blessings from Him when I pray for people.

I had prayed a lot and for days getting ready for my invitation to speak at Hankerman Community Church. I didn't have any speaking experience what so ever. This date was the following weekend after the Lord multiplied the oil in my bottle. The day came and they called my name. I could feel the Holy Spirit with me as I began to speak. I may be six foot six, but when I feel His presence with me tears run down my cheeks. Sometimes that makes it hard for me to speak at all. Connie asked me once to pray and ask God to help me stop crying when I speak. I quickly responded by telling her no, I will not do that. Little children and adults see the big man cry and I am not ashamed. The Lord knows what I need. I began to speak, telling many stories that you have read so far and some others as well. I knew the Lord was with me and I shared for thirty minutes. All of a sudden, known only to me, the Lord said, "Tell them about the oil and stop." I said, "Folks, I have one more story to tell you then my friend Cary is going to sing the song, *Make My Life a Bible*." When Connie heard I was going to tell about the oil, she told me later that she scooted down in her seat in the back of the church. Remember, when we both witnessed the full bottle she asked me not to tell anyone. She said no one would believe it if they had not seen it. Connie did not know at the time that the Lord had told me to testify about it. No matter what, I was going to share it. I took the bottle out and set it on the podium and it was still full. I had only prayed for four people since the Lord had multiplied it. I shared the story.

I told the congregation that there were two things I wanted them to know. First, I would not meet Jesus lying about the oil. The second, I would not take a million dollars for that little bottle of oil, but I would give it away one drop at a time.

I stepped off the platform and Cary Gilham started singing, *Make My Life a Bible*. The anointing in that room was overwhelming and people started coming out of the pews and lining up all around me at the altar, to receive prayer with oil from that bottle. The line went all the way to the back door. It was beautiful and everyone was blessed.

When everyone was prayed for and it was time to go home, Perry said, "John, I have never seen anything like this in all the years that I have been coming here." I told him neither had I, and I was just glad to be a small part of it. It was all God.

To this day, I do not know if Perry knew that was my first service. I collected my Bible, cowboy hat and began to look for my wife. It took me awhile to find her; I think she was hiding under a pew. We started out the door and Connie walked out ahead of me. I had one arm and one foot out when someone grabbed me and pulled me back in. It was brother Lynn and he said they wanted to give me some money. I said, "I don't take money." He started telling me about the price of gas and all of the other reasons I should take the money.

I kept telling him no, and we went back and forth until the Lord reminded me what He showed me about the two hundred dollars four days earlier. I knew what Lynn was going to say before he said it. He said the amount he had to give me was two hundred dollars. "Okay! I have already been talked to about it." He asked who talked to me about it. I told him the Holy Spirit had and He already showed me what to do with it. I then asked him if he had any hurricane Rita evacuees at his church. He said he did. I then told him he was to keep one hundred of it to feed them, and I would take the other hundred to the First Baptist Church in Kountze. I told him they had three hundred in the city to feed. He thought that was a great idea I had, but the idea did not come from me.

The Home the Hurricane Spared

While I was at Hankerman Community Church, a man named Rodney approached me and asked if I would anoint a house. This was a house he had used for ministry. He informed me it was a retreat for evangelists and people of God who needed a quiet place to rest. This was the first building I had anointed and this was prior to hurricane Rita. We did not know at the time that this area was going to take a great hit from the hurricane along with my city and home in seven days. We knew the hurricane was out there, but did not know the devastation it would bring on its way. I went with him and anointed the home with oil on the main entrance of the door, and asked the Lord's blessing on it. We dedicated all of it to God.

That house lost only one shingle in that storm. The homes surrounding it were devastated. Rodney jokingly told me later that we should have anointed the trees, too. All of the trees that surrounded that house were lying flat. He then thanked me and prayed for me. I don't care who you are, we all need prayer. You give Him your inside and He will take care of your outside. He will change you as you yield instead of you trying to change yourself, but it is always a matter of choice.

Healing is Useless without Salvation

The Lord started leading me to begin my prayers with others in a certain way. He directed me to approach His Throne by first asking for forgiveness for our sins, whether it is in our words, thoughts or deeds. We should have a clean slate before we petition for requests. I began to see more and more salvations in the healing prayer groups I was invited to.

I was praying for a healing for a man named Butch. During that prayer two people received Christ, Butch's friend and his eleven year old grandson. Healing is temporary in the fact that we all will eventually die someday. What eternal good is it to have our physical bodies healed if our soul does not belong to Jesus? The reality of life is that after we die, we will either go to Heaven or hell. There is only one way to Heaven and that is through Jesus Christ, accepting Him as our Lord and Savior. Jesus came in the flesh and died on our behalf so we could be reconciled to God from our sin. He leaves the choice to us. All of our good deeds will not earn our way into Heaven, neither will just believing He exists. Even the demons believe and know that. We have to invite Him to be the Lord of our life through prayer. We have to have an ongoing relationship with Him.

In Matthew, the Bible says that not everyone who says "Lord" on that day will enter in. He will tell many that He never "knew" them. A onetime sinner's prayer does not cut it. It is our journey with Him from that point on, until the day we are called home. We can't just be sorry for our sins, but we have to repent from them and change our mind and our direction. It's not about having religion with a convenient fire insurance policy that keeps us out of hell. Simply calling on Him only when we're in trouble or thinking that one prayer for salvation is all we need is not enough.

It's a permanent change in us to follow Him for the rest of our living days. John 3:16 -17, "For God so greatly loved and dearly prized the world that He [even] gave up His only begotten (unique) Son, so that whoever believes in (trusts in, clings to, relies on) Him shall not perish (come to destruction, be lost) but have eternal (everlasting) life. For God did not send the Son into the world in order to judge (to reject, to condemn, to pass sentence on) the world, but that the world might find salvation and be made safe and sound through Him."

Therefore, it is clear to me that there are two reasons the Lord leads me to pray for people: Healing and salvation. Jesus died for both. It was by His stripes (wounds) that we were healed (Isaiah 53: 5). There is no doubt that no matter what situation you are in, being saved is more important than being healed. Eternity in hell is a long time compared to the short time we are on Earth. As hard as it would be, I would rather lose a child at birth, than to raise it just to lose him or her to Satan. God loves us because we are His creation and made in His image. He does not want any of us to perish. Again, we have free will and the choice is ours to make. Satan does not mind if we have a little bit or a lot of religion, as long as we don't have a relationship with Jesus.

Religion is manmade and will not "save" you. When we receive Christ, the Holy Spirit resides in us and enables us with His power to live for Jesus. Salvation is not a great mystery, anyone can have it. There is enough gospel in John 3:16 to save the world, it is a Bible within itself. The Book of Revelation is almost fulfilled, be ready to meet Him!

Religion is man's attempt to earn their way into Heaven by following rules, rituals and doing good deeds (working your way into Heaven). Religion has different doctrines and can be confusing

Healing is Useless without Salvation

because each one is different. That is why you have to base your life on the Word of God, the Holy Bible. A personal relationship with Jesus and following Him is what reserves our place in Heaven. Satan's biggest tool is deception, he does not want you to know this or believe this. His battlefield is our mind. Like I said, he doesn't mind if you stay religious, he just does not want you to open up your Bible or your mouth to pray because things change and start to happen when you do that. Your mind becomes renewed (changed) and your heart and actions will follow. You have a direct line to God when you pray. You don't have to go through a pastor or priest to have God hear you and answer you when you talk to Him. Once you are saved, He sees the blood of Jesus on you and you can approach His throne with boldness!

We do not know what tomorrow holds for any of us. You could be gone tomorrow. If you are not sure if you are saved or not, or if you have backslid and want to make things right with the Lord, read the following prayer aloud:

SINNER'S PRAYER

Lord Jesus, thank You for dying on the cross so that my sins would be forgiven. I ask You to forgive all of my sins in thoughts, words and deeds. I know You shed Your blood for my salvation. I accept this free gift. I ask You now to live in me, guide me and have a relationship with me. Reveal Yourself to me in a personal way and help me to know Your voice. Teach me in Your Word how to live my life in a way that is pleasing to You. Change me to be the person that You created me to be. I surrender my life to You now. I ask You to help me in every area of my life. Redeem my mistakes and give my life meaning and eternal value. I pray this in faith believing You have heard me and will answer me. I thank You for loving me enough to die for me. Amen.

If you prayed this prayer with a sincere heart, He has heard you and the angels in Heaven are rejoicing. Your life will never be the same again if you follow Him. Life will still have its hardships and heartaches, but He will walk with you every step of the way and give you victory through it all.

Ask Him to reveal His purpose for you and His plan for your life, no matter what age you are at now. You are never too old for Him to use you and do amazing things with your life. It is a process and we can enjoy the journey even in difficult times, because we know that He has good plans for us. Jeremiah 29:11, "For I know the thoughts and plans that I have for you, says the Lord, thoughts and plans for welfare and peace and not for evil, to give you hope in your final outcome." Romans 8:28, "We are assured and know that [God being a partner in their labor] all things work together and are [fitting into a plan] for good to and for those who love God and are called according to [His] design and purpose."

To the church, God has a message for us too. It is time for us to wake up out of our complacency and apathy, and re-light the fire for Him for our redemption draws near. He is coming back soon! We are either cold or hot for His kingdom, there is no middle ground. Revelation 3:16, "So, because you are lukewarm and neither cold nor hot, I will spew you out of My mouth!" Ouch, that one hurts. We can't fake it until we make it or just go through the motions. He knows our heart.

Again, in Matthew 7: 21-23, He says, "Not everyone who says to Me, Lord, Lord, will enter the kingdom of heaven, but he who does the will of My Father who is in Heaven. 22 Many will say to Me on that day, Lord, Lord, have we not prophesied in Your name and driven out demons in Your name and done many mighty works in Your name? 23 And then I will say to them openly (publicly), I never knew you; depart from Me, you who act wickedly [disregarding my commands]." The "never knew" part means we never had a personal relationship with Him, we just had our religion, programs and rituals. That is a pretty powerful verse.

The Bible says in the end times even the elect (that's you and me) will be deceived (Matthew 24: 24). Religious activity is not a substitute for living according to the will and ways of God. God is love but He won't be mocked. He can't go against His Word, it is spiritual law. So, believers need to look at their spiritual condition too, as well as the unsaved. Satan is the deceiver. We must always be alert to his schemes in our thoughts that make us complacent and fall out of relationship with Jesus.

It is vital for our growth to be plugged in with other believers and a Bible teaching church. This is how we grow in our walk with Him, otherwise we are prey. You know you are in the right church when you hear the Holy Spirit talking to your spirit through the message. It will speak directly to you and your life. The Bible says not to forsake the gathering of the brethren. This is for several reasons. We need to hear the Word to know Him and to grow. A pastor who listens to God will receive a revelation from Him to share with us. It will speak to our present circumstances. Fellowship keeps us encouraged, accountable and on the right track. Bad company corrupts good character. We need the influence of other believers in our lives just like our kids need good friendships to keep them on the right course. The Bible refers to the church as His "bride" and He is the "groom." A bride and groom are intimate and spend time together, which is how their relationship flourishes and grows. The Bible promises that once we belong to Him, He will never leave us nor forsake us. If anyone leaves, it is us leaving Him.

Therefore, it is clear to me that there are two reasons the Lord has me pray for people. Healing is one, but the most important reason is salvation. You can know "about" Him without "knowing" Him. Salvation is the greatest miracle known to man.

The Hitchhiker

In today's world I do not pick up hitchhikers, but one day I did. I was coming out of Buna, Texas, and Rita had torn up the whole gulf coast. My next stop was at the bank in Lumberton, about six miles away. I saw a hitchhiker out of the corner of my eye; only saw an image of a person. I did not understand it, but the next thing I knew my foot hit the brake and I was pulling over to the side of the road. It was like someone else was driving. Then a man got into my truck, he needed a bath last week, never mind today. His hair was down to his hips and we said our pleasantries.

As I was driving along the highway I was wondering what this was about. I already knew it was something greater than myself that made me stop. The man started talking and telling me many things and none of it was good. His every other word was a cuss word and then he apologized for his bad language. That was my opening, "I don't judge you, that's between you and the Lord. Some Christians tend to judge and gossip when they think they are right with God. I do not do that. I have also done many things in my life. I have not murdered, raped or pillaged, but I have broken many of the commandments."

The man asked if I was a preacher. I told him no, I am just a man who testifies what God has done for me and I pray for people. Nothing in my past compares to what He is doing in my life now. He proceeded to tell me that he was Catholic. I told him I was nondenominational. However, the Lord had me on the radio praying for all denominations for a year and a half. I then told him the story of how the Lord had me pray for a Franciscan priest, ten Catholics and two Baptists before we went live on the air.

I shared with him how I was trying to live and that there was a song that really was a prayer put into music, *Make My Life a Bible*. This song describes my life goal and what I want to achieve in my walk with Christ. I then played the song for him and the presence of God entered my truck.

I arrived at my destination at the bank and parked. I said to him, "This is as far as I go." My passenger said this had helped him out a lot and he wanted to thank me. He went on to say that was the prettiest song that he had ever heard in his life. I told him it was the same for me. I handed him a copy of the song and my card. He shook my hand and got out. He then walked around to my side of the truck and shook my hand again. I told him that I wished there was more that I could do for him. He said I had no idea what I had already done and thanked me again.

The last time I saw him, he was walking down highway 69 with tears running down his cheeks and holding a copy of the song, *Make My Life a Bible*. I then felt the Holy Spirit's presence one more time.

Aggie and the Angel

One day in 2002, my mother asked me if I wanted the little angel she had in her jewelry box. An angel made out of pure gold, small, but pure gold all the same. I asked her where that angel had come from. She said Aggie had given it to her many years ago. I remember Aggie from my childhood. Aggie was a small person with many birth defects. She always had a smile on her face and was always doing something for others when she herself had nothing. I remembered her example she had on others all of these years. She was a true Christian and I thought of her often.

Here we are 50 years later, and I was wearing that angel on my cowboy hat. I thought no more about it after I pinned it there.

One night I walked into a store in the country. The man and wife running the store were from the Middle East. When I walked up to the counter he asked me about the beautiful angel. I knew then that Aggie's angel had a job to do after being in a box for 50 years. I then told him about the story of the woman who was small but great. I told him that angel was a token of Christian friendship and it was priceless to me. As he stared at it for a moment he then looked at me and said, "Money means nothing, it is people who matter." Tears began to run down my face and I was not ashamed. I could tell it had an impact on him.

As time passed, the Lord led me to a woman who almost cried when I told her the story of Aggie and the angel. I did not want to do it, but the Lord told me, "Give it to her!" I did. That really took her back that I did that; tears started running down her cheeks and I never saw her again. It wasn't the angel pin in itself that got people's attention, it was the Holy Spirit using it to draw their heart to Jesus. The anointing on it made it a magnet.

God can use small things, He can use anything to reach out to someone.

Mistreated as a Child

Then there was Gladys. Gladys was elderly and I knew it was close to her time. I was asked to pray with her so I went to see her. She was a Christian Catholic and you would have never met a better person. She was struggling with many issues. A family member had somehow taken thousands of dollars away from her. The details I do not know however, Gladys had a lot of stress and resentment.

She had also been mistreated as a child by certain family members. The abuse went on throughout her life, yet Gladys raised children that were not her own and prayed to the Lord every day. She then began to ask for me on a regular basis. I saw her at least two times a week and we prayed together every time. The Holy Spirit helped Gladys lay everything down until she had total forgiveness for everyone who caused all of the anguish in her life. In the process, I asked her to pray for me every day when she recited her rosary. She prayed for me every day after that. I gave her some music and she began to love it. *Make My Life a Bible* and *Storms Never Last* became her favorites. Her husband and son took care of her in their home to the very end. When she passed, she was at total peace. It is important to note that four days before Gladys passed, she would not turn her rosary loose.

I was asked to speak at her funeral and considered it an honor and privilege. After the priest spoke, it was my turn and I will never forget it. I had prayed prior for the presence of the Holy Spirit to be there when I spoke. Praise God He showed up in a powerful way and I could barely contain myself. They played *Make My Life a Bible* and *Storms Never Last*. I spoke that day to every denomination and to people that had no church connections that I knew about.

Afterward, the priest approached me and commended me. One of the things I spoke about was salvation. I told them that if they did not know if they were saved or not to see their priest, pastor or clergy. I then told them if they did not want to do that, then please see me. I am no one special, but I can show you the path to Jesus.

Prayer Posse for Jesus

In keeping with my philosophy that I am not the only one who can pray, I asked several people to join me in prayer for a lady named Sandra. We are supposed to be an army for Christ, to battle in prayer when the enemy tries to impose his plans for us over the plans and purposes of God. Like I said, I call it forming a posse for Jesus. One year in March I heard from Sandra, it had been months prior when we had prayed for her. She informed me that the chronic pain we had prayed about was totally gone. I never cease to get excited when the Lord answers prayers and I see it often. You can't get that high off of drugs and alcohol. It doesn't get any better than this.

All Their Prayers Answered

We prayed for a lady named Andrea, a young woman who had heart problems and wasn't expected to live long. We also prayed for Max and his wife Delores, who were overwhelmed with stress in their family. Max was known to pray for people who had demonic spirits tormenting them, so Satan was trying to take him out any way he could. One night we gathered and prayed for all of these needs.

I got a call one day in November and was told that every prayer request that we prayed over that night had been answered, every single one and that was a first for me. We were all amazed by this and gave thanks to the Lord. Most of these people that were prayed for that night went to the same church. After hearing that all prayers were answered they shut the church service down that following Sunday. We gathered in a classroom just to share with each other what the Lord had done for them in a week's time.

Isaiah 53:5, "But He was wounded for our transgressions, He was bruised for our guilt and iniquities; the chastisement [needful to obtain] peace and well-being for us was upon Him, and with the stripes [that wounded] Him we are healed and made whole."

Healing pertains to much more than physical healing. Healing also applies to our emotional hurts, stress, unforgiveness we can't overcome, affects from abuse, and every part in us that is broken.

Eight Polygraph Truths

The man I am about to tell you about went through a horror worse than death. Being a Christian, death was preferred. Every family member he had turned against him. The Lord sent him to me. There are no coincidences with God. Proverbs 16:33, "The lot is cast into the lap, but the decision is wholly of the Lord [even events that seem accidental are really ordered by Him]." God paves the way if we are diligently following Him.

This man was accused of molesting two of his grandchildren and was afraid he might go to jail for something that never happened. He had beautiful relationships with them and now they were being destroyed. After the worse accusation ever, he lost eighteen pounds and was unable to sleep much. He spent hours on his face asking God to reveal any and all things he may have done wrong. His heartache was unbearable. This was multiplied by the fact that not one family member believed that he was innocent and he was completely cut off from his grandchildren.

The church that he attended, were the only people who believed he had not abused these children or anyone else. The strain was so overwhelming that he actually collapsed from the stress.

He took a polygraph test. The man conducting the test had been doing polygraphs for forty years. He told the accused man that he would back him up one hundred percent that he was telling the truth. There was some relief having this person believe him. Some of his family members believed the test, others said he was lying and beat the test.

Please take note of these eight truths:

1. Satan is the accuser of man, not God.
2. False accusers are as guilty as the one who supposedly did the crime.
3. The accused person must work through anger, pain, anguish, grief, loneliness and heartache.
4. God can help you through any crisis, no matter how bad it is. There are many promises in His Word that can sustain you and lift you up, and renew your spirit daily. Read them and pray them out loud, this increases our faith.
5. If you are honest before God, He will reveal truth to you by the power of the Holy Spirit.
6. The truth may never be known to others, at least in this world.
7. The Lord knows the truth of the matter. He knows who really abused the children if it happened at all. Children today see graphic things in books, movies, magazines, computers or watching it on television. They can transfer these images to a person, especially if they are coaxed by the right person.
8. Anyone who has been falsely accused needs to spend time alone each day with the Lord and their Bible, to hear Him speak to their spirit.

Why did I believe he was innocent? First, he passed the polygraph test. Second, he was one of the most kind hearted and sensitive persons I have ever met. He came to me for prayer; he could not hang on much longer. He asked that this whole burden and situation be lifted off of his shoulders.

Folks, I formed a prayer group for this man with a group of Christians who believed him. We all laid hands on him and prayed. The Holy Spirit showed up in such a strong way that he almost collapsed again. The weight was lifted and he felt relief. We knew the Lord was going to vindicate him. The Bible says that God is our vindicator. I told him that I knew he was not guilty, otherwise the

Holy Spirit would not have shown up like He did. He thanked the Lord for lifting the weight off of his shoulders and he felt freedom from the oppression that was trying to crush him. The Lord God alone gets the glory.

A lot of men have been falsely accused and released from prison in the last several years because of advanced DNA tests. One man served forty years for a murder he did not commit.

We need to watch what we say about people. We will have to answer to God one day for the things we have said and done to other people. The Lord cares about everything that concerns us. Psalm 138:8, "The Lord will perfect that which concerns me. Your mercy and loving-kindness, O Lord, endure forever—forsake not the work of your own hands." This pertains to every aspect of our life. Psalm 40:2, "He drew me up out of a horrible pit [a pit of tumult and of destruction]. Out of the miry clay (froth and slime), and set my feet upon a rock, steadying my steps and establishing my goings."

God cares about our stress, our relationships, our finances, our heart's desires, just as much as He cares when we are physically ill. He wants us to give Him our hurtful memories of our past and regrets, and let Him heal the emotional wounds. His Word is like a healing balm when read consistently with prayer.

Again, prayer is a two way communication. We talk and we listen. He has different ways of answering us. He will put people in our path that can help us with our needs. He will give us thoughts or ideas, a revelation on how to handle a situation. He will guide us when we are seeking a direction to take in a certain area.

You will be reading your Bible as I said before, and an answer will fly off the page to you. Don't be so quick to judge others; you have been forgiven of much. Joyce Meyer says, "Hurting people hurt other people." Extend grace and forgiveness to others as often as you can. That is exactly what Christ did for you. If we don't forgive each other and harbor it, then our prayers are hindered.

It is the goodness of God that draws people to the house of God. We should not be self-righteous, judgmental, critical, or arrogant towards others. Only God can judge and convict a person. We push people away from God when we treat them that way.

You don't have to hang around someone who hurts you, but your heart has to forgive them. Anger in itself isn't wrong, it is how we deal with it. Anger is a God given emotion that signals to us that something is wrong. Sometimes we need to confront someone; sometimes it is best that we don't. God will give you discernment on that. It is imperative though that we confess our sins so we can be forgiven. Forgiveness is the main message of the cross. You have heard it said before, unforgiveness just puts you in a prison. It is like drinking poison and hoping someone else dies. Sometimes we are called to forgive and reconcile with that person, other times we are called to forgive and walk away. God never wants us in a position where someone is causing us harm or is abusing us. He is the judge and vindicator. He will handle your enemies and vengeance is His alone, just hand it all over to Him. There is power in the name of Jesus; we should pray our prayers in the name of Jesus. There is no name above that Name. There is power in the blood of Jesus. We should plead the blood of Jesus over ourselves, loved ones and situations. We have straight access to the throne through Jesus. That is our blood bought right. The Bible says at the name of Jesus, everything in Heaven and earth must bow.

The battle between Heaven and hell was won the day Jesus was crucified. Until Jesus comes back we will still battle with evil, because Satan still roams the Earth until his judgment day. God has given us authority to use the name of Jesus to fight our earthly battles. Satan and his demons will be thrown into the lake of fire (hell – Revelation 19: 20).

In the meantime, Satan wants to take as many of us with him as possible. We don't have to like, approve, or associate with everyone, but we are held accountable for how we treat them. People should see love in us if we are true followers of Christ, because God is love. That does not make us a door mat for people to mistreat us. We have the right to say no and to be bold when standing up for what is right and what is wrong. We should always maintain our boundaries with others.

Bitterness and resentments are the same as unforgiveness. These areas are the baits of Satan. He knows if he can keep us locked up in these emotions, then we are ineffective for God and we will not be able to move forward. We will remain stuck and it will contaminate us and everyone around us. Sometimes we can't forgive in our own strength, that is when we give it to Him and the emotions will follow later. We don't wait until our emotions "feel" like it first. Emotions are fickle and can be deceiving as well.

Whatever measure we use to judge others, will be the same measure used to judge us. God is the only One who has the power to change others in the first place, and He is the One who has the power to change us.

Miracles Continue

The Lord said, "I have not spoken yet." Laura asked me to go to the hospital to pray for a young lady who was twenty-eight years old. She was in the intensive care unit with blood clots in her lungs and other places in her body. Debbie had many health problems. Laura and I left to go to the hospital and when we got there she introduced me to Bertha, Debbie's mother. The three of us gathered in the waiting room and prayed. All of us went into Debbie's room. She was not conscious. The three of us began to pray again. We felt the Holy Spirit's presence in the room.

My friend Tony stopped by one day and asked if I would go to the hospital and pray for several people. I immediately said yes as I was getting ready to go myself. We prayed for all of the people that Tony knew in the hospital and then headed to Debbie's room to pray for her some more. We visited with Bertha and she said things were not looking good. She was still unconscious and that was on a Wednesday.

That following Sunday I visited Tony's church and asked him how Debbie was doing. I told him that I had received a call the night before and was informed that her doctors didn't think she was going to make it. Her organs were starting to shut down. I did not mention to him that the Lord had spoken to me to go pray for her again and again. The Lord spoke to my spirit that the doctors had spoken, but He had not. So I kept going back to pray for her. I had not met

Debbie prior to her being in the hospital. One day she regained consciousness and spoke to me. I kept going back and then she began to ask for me. Before long, Debbie was out of intensive care and in a regular room. We began to visit and I brought her some music to listen to. The first CD I gave her was, *Make my Life a Bible*. By this time I think she was trying to figure out why I was coming to see her all of the time. I was not an ordained preacher or even a deacon in the church. I told her about the job the Lord had given me and about the first time He had sent me to pray for someone. I shared with her how He blessed my efforts and obedience by healing many of the people I had prayed for. I told her about the miracles I had seen and how He in turn, blessed me in so many ways. I told her that being a prayer warrior was part selfish, because He allowed the Holy Spirit to descend on me as well as the others in our prayer groups.

I have learned to soak in the presence of the Holy Spirit. I always look forward to the next time, like a kid at Christmas anxiously waiting.

Soon Debbie was walking a few feet until she finally walked out of the room. She started walking farther and farther. Fifty feet, seventy feet, and it kept progressing until she walked right out of that hospital. Now, the Lord had spoken!

I got a call one day from a man nicknamed "Bubba" who had liver cancer. We prayed until I got another call that all spots on his liver were gone.

My daughter-in-law, Jamie, wanted prayer for her friend Theresa's father, Carl. He was being rushed to the hospital for a heart attack. Connie, Jamie, my grandson and I prayed for him. We nicknamed my grandson "Taylor Tot" and he was under a year old at the time, but we figured we might as well get him accustomed to praying early in life. Carl was still in route to the hospital when we prayed. Three minutes after entering the emergency room, Carl's heart valve opened. They sent him home the next morning.

I never get tired seeing the miracles and I thank the Lord for letting me be a small part of it. Like the day I went to see my mother, a friend of the family Joann was there along with her fifteen year old son. He had a heart condition and Joann wanted a new job. God came through for her big time. Her son was totally healed and can play sports with his friends. She got a new job paying five dollars more an hour.

One day I was looking through the Sunday paper and noticed only one store promoting a Christmas sale instead of a Holiday sale. That store was Kohls in Beaumont, so I drove there to buy some jewelry for Connie. Christmas was bearing down on me and I liked the fact that the store was not trying to abort Christ out of Christmas. Pastor Tony Thornton called me on my cell phone and we were in the process of looking for someone to sing at our special church services. I was standing at the counter as we talked when the lady behind the counter overheard our conversation. She was an attractive lady named Linda. She spoke up and asked for prayer right then and there. She had breast cancer. I took her hand and prayed and felt the Spirit with us. The people in the store who were standing around the counter waited patiently and quietly. I never did hear the outcome of Linda and her illness. I mention this because I want people to see how often the Lord sets me up with people who need prayer. I was set up to go to Kohls in the first place. I hope she was healed. I believe she was because the Lord sent me there.

The Lord is constantly sending me people when I least expect it. That is okay, because I am always ready. I am always ready because I stay prayed up and ask the Holy Spirit to stay with me. He always comes through no matter how difficult things get. When I pray for a lot of people back to back I get tired and drained of energy, until I rest up and am ready to go again. This is because of the overpowering presence of the Holy Spirit in my life. Do not misunderstand me though, I would keep praying for people even if it killed me. This is not a complaint, just a fact.

I remember awhile back I was in Louisiana attending the funeral of Kenneth McCready. His wife Billie Dee is my first cousin. Afterwards we went to a restaurant to grab a bite to eat. Martha, Billie and myself were there, all of us first cousins. The restaurant only had four or five other people eating there and it was close to closing time. I had on my big western hat and suit. We were halfway through our meal when a very well dressed man approached our table. He asked me if I had a horse to go with that suit. I looked up and replied, "Yes I do," and handed him my card. On the card was a picture of my beautiful stallion that the Lord had blessed me with. The words, "Have prayer, will travel" were also on the card along with a gold cross. The man looked at the card and said, "I was supposed to go to another place to eat tonight, but the Lord sent me here. Now I know why. I am supposed to ask you to pray for me and my wife." The meal was no longer important. I inquired where his wife was and he said she was out in the car. "Let's go," I said and without hesitation we headed out the door.

I left my two cousins in the restaurant to finish their meal. Out in the parking lot there were only a few cars and no other people around. He took me to his black Lincoln. The car had more chrome than I had ever seen on an automobile. When he opened the door on the passenger's side, I saw that his wife had braces on her legs. I introduced myself and we both prayed for her. I then turned to her husband and said, "Inside you asked for prayer for your wife and yourself. What do you need prayer for?" "Stress!" he said. He then told me that the judge and lawyers here in town took two and a half million dollars from him that he had set aside for a children's center. I told him that I did not doubt him and we began to pray. The Holy Spirit rained down on us in a mighty way right there in the parking lot.

After the prayer the man said, "I have ten acres of land in the city and I am going to build the most beautiful church that anyone has ever seen." I told him if he did that, I would come and help him open the doors that first day. Texas was not that far away and I would look forward to it. He said I would be there when that happens. When I returned to the restaurant my cousin was concerned and wondered how I could go out to the parking lot with a man I did not know. She could not believe I did that. I told Martha that was the easiest question anyone has ever asked me. I felt the spirit of the man from the moment he walked up to the table. I knew it was God that brought him there.

Make my life a Bible Lord, make my life a Bible. May they see You and not me.

God Rewards Faithfulness

One day I was at church when the pastor's wife Judy asked me and four other people to pray with her in the office before the service started. She had something on her heart that she felt led to pray about. Sister Judy started praying first and we took turns as we stood in a circle. She caught me off guard when she started praying for me to be rewarded for the work I was doing for the Lord. She prayed quite a while for me and then started praying for the situation she was burdened about. The other people prayed and then it was my turn.

This is what I prayed, "Lord, I want that reward and this is what I want. I am asking You to answer the prayers I pray for Your people that you send into my life, and that it would be for your glory, that would be the only thing I want."

Things really picked up after that. I was praying for more and more people. Within a few weeks my wife was blessed with a beautiful Overo Paint colt. People far and wide came to see him.

In 2006, Warrior turned four years old. We then started breeding other people's mares. I have had horses for over 50 years. This gift from God was the first horse to make money. I praise the Lord for that reward. I have often thought of King Solomon after seeing all that happened after receiving Warrior. I had asked for blessings for the Lord's people, not anything for myself. People always come first. However, the Lord did not forget me. Warrior has caused many people to come to know the Lord. Solomon only asked God for wisdom. God not only answered that prayer, but added many blessings for him as well. People would come to see Warrior and sometimes ask for prayer, and the Holy Spirit would show up in that barn with us. Under normal circumstances, Connie and I would never be able to afford a horse off of a millionaire's ranch. The Lord worked it out for us to keep him. We now had the most beautiful horse we had ever seen. Only God can make things like that happen.

One day I had plans to go to the hospital and pray for someone. As soon as I got out of bed and my feet hit the floor, I knew I was sick. Not just a little bit sick, head plugged, sore throat and you name it. I put on my robe and headed for the kitchen. I didn't think I would enjoy my coffee because I felt so bad. As I walked I prayed, just as if the Lord was walking with me. "Lord, if you want me to go to the hospital and pray for this person then You will have to first heal me. I can't go pray for the sick if I am sick myself." In three more strides I had reached the coffee pot. I picked up a cup and started pouring the coffee, and as it was pouring I knew I was totally healed. Without a doubt I knew the Lord wanted me to go to that hospital and pray for someone.

I then left to go pray for the person who had asked for me. She had been sick for two years. She had felt bad for so long that her family didn't believe that she was sick anymore. Her self-worth was at an all-time low. She had spent several nights at the beach in their van and no one knew where she was. She was now so sick that she ended up in the hospital again. She wanted to get well or die. I remember that we had prayed for a change of doctors, knowing she needed a specialist to accurately diagnose her. They were going to run more tests on her that afternoon so we prayed for a diagnosis.

The next day God answered her prayer. She was diagnosed with Crohn's disease. It is a chronic condition where inflammation causes injury to the intestines. We gave praise to the Lord for a long awaited answer. We continued to pray for this situation and the Lord continued to answer prayers as He has promised. She became close to her family again. All credit goes to the Lord for delivering this lady.

God has many names in the Bible that refer to His characteristics. Jehovah Rapha means God, our Healer.

God Rewards Faithfulness

After leaving her room that day I stood by the elevator and was approached by a black man I did not know. I don't care what a person's race is, I love them all. Wearing my western attire he assumed correctly that I might have a horse. It seemed he loved horses and we began to discuss mine. We ended the conversation by me inviting him to my home. He then turned away and walked down the hall. The elevator opened and I stepped in. I met another lady and began to talk to her. The conversation continued outside the elevator on the ground floor. She was a perfect stranger, but I love to talk to God's people and I will talk to anyone. I proceeded to the main entrance. The hospital was new and I did not know there was a chapel on the first floor. Just as I was walking past the stained glass doors, they opened. Out of the doors came the same man I was speaking to by the elevator upstairs. Since I already considered him a friend I said, "What are you stealing in there?" His reply made me feel really bad. He said, "No! I was in there praying for my uncle. He is very sick and they are going to do a procedure on him that is supposed to be bad. I was praying for him." I began to give him my testimony on healing, a few stories like the ones you have already read. He promptly invited me to go back upstairs to pray for his uncle and upstairs we went. Wouldn't you know we were right next door to the lady's room that I had prayed for earlier. I met his mother and his sister. The man needing prayer looked bad. I was almost afraid to pray for him. He was not conscious. This can only be described as a lack of faith on my part. However I did say to the family, "I know that sometimes God's healing is death." I have never said that again, especially after what followed. I asked everyone in the room to come lay hands on that man. We prayed and the presence of the Holy Spirit was overwhelming. Then I was asked to pray for each of them in the room. Once again, I asked all other believers to pray for each one with me. I am not the only one that the Lord wants to hear from. I did not know that the man I met at the elevator and was talking to about horses was a preacher.

Remember, I started out that day to pray for one person, now there were five. Remember also, I started out that morning sick myself and was healed at my coffee pot. However, I absolutely do know the Lord God knows all, past, present, and future. Jesus ministered to my needs that day so that I was able to minister and pray for His people.

The next day I got a call from a member of his family. It seems that within two hours after I had left, his uncle was sitting up and watching television. The doctors canceled the painful procedure and he was discharged from the hospital that following morning. His family told him what had taken place. We gave thanks and praise to the Lord on the phone. My God, only You can do something like this. You are the one true God and there is no other.

I am not perfect and I make mistakes. I am human. I, like everyone else around me wonders why God allows me to get sick while I am out praying for healing for His people. Everything has a reason and a purpose. I have been sick with a bug for the last two days. During the short time at the doctor's office and getting an x-ray, I was given the opportunity to testify and share what the Lord has done to at least fifteen people. Yes, I believe the Lord had that planned. In Proverbs 3:5, the Bible says that His ways are not our ways and we can't lean on our own understanding. I still thank Him for letting me be a small part of His big plans.

The Holy Spirit

The Holy Spirit is the third person in the Trinity. He is the unseen but ever present all powerful divine Spirit of God. Jesus said He would send the Holy Spirit to us just prior to Him being crucified. The Holy Spirit resides in you the moment you ask Jesus Christ to be your Savior. He was sent to Earth when Jesus left to be our guide, counselor and comforter.

The Holy Spirit is God's presence here on Earth and can be felt by believers when we seek God. He woos unbelievers to the knowledge of Christ. Jesus goes to the Father (God) on our behalf when we pray. That is why we pray in the name of Jesus. We activate the Holy Spirit in our lives when our walk with the Lord is evident in our life. He is an actual person.

The Holy Trinity consists of God, Jesus, and the Holy Spirit. They operate as One. He is as real as the people you actually see. He is the power of God and is every Christian's weapon against Satan and his works. John 10:10, "The thief (Satan) comes only in order to steal and kill and destroy. I came that they may have and enjoy life, and have it in abundance (to the full, till it overflows)." We tap into the power of the Holy Spirit when we speak and pray God's Word which is alive and active, and when we worship and give our praise.

Worship is the highest form of prayer. Every time Jesus took a stripe (beating) we were saved, healed and delivered from something (Isaiah 53: 5). He paid for our freedom that day and left us the keys to the kingdom. We have to actively pick up those keys and access what He died to give us. He gave us authority over the enemy when we live by and use His principles and speak His Word. When we worship Jesus, the Holy Spirit is always present. God's presence inhabits the praises of His people. Satan wants to be worshiped, so he hates it when we worship God. He flees the scene when we worship, just like he has to flee when we use or call on the name of Jesus.

The Holy Spirit guides us and gives us revelation to all truth about God, and about us and our circumstances. When we are searching for an answer or a promise to our situation, He is the one who speaks to us in our spirit and through the Word of God. He is literally God's presence on Earth. Since He is the power and breath of God, He is present every time a miracle or salvation takes place. We can have as much of Him or as little of Him as we want. It is our choice. He will not go where He is not wanted or welcomed.

The anointing is the power of the Holy Spirit working in our lives. The anointing is the burden removing, yoke destroying power of God. When the Holy Spirit is there, the anointing is there and that is the atmosphere where supernatural miracles take place. The anointing is the divine enabling, God's ability on our ability enabling us to do what we can't do on our own. God calls us His anointed ones. The anointing is evident through peace, joy, and sometimes tears of release. It is the exact opposite of heaviness, oppression, and depression.

Yielding to the leading of the Holy Spirit in all areas of your life means that you stop and allow Him to guide you. He will speak to your spirit and give you insight, revelation and wisdom. You follow His leading and not go ahead of Him. He can get you where you need to be. We shouldn't make decisions based just on opinions or experiences, but by the leading of the Spirit. Some of us don't learn that lesson until we have come to the end of our rope and have exhausted our flesh, and our own resources.

The Holy Spirit works through believers to answer the prayers of God's people. He will send the right people in your path at the right time to aid you. When we meditate on His Word (Bible), we are infused with the knowledge and power needed to accomplish all things. He speaks to us through numerous ways. Again, He speaks

The Holy Spirit

through the Word; sometimes words will fly off the page and talk directly to us, through people, through a sudden thought or idea. Our spirit will recognize when it is Him speaking. If any answer comes to us that does not line up with the Word of God, then it is not from Him. We are to use discernment when we want to hear from Him and make sure it is confirmed by our spirit, and not from our flesh and what it wants.

There is a constant battle between our flesh and our spirit. The flesh will always want to do things its own way. His Spirit has no boundaries. He can speak through a pastor, friend, a message we hear, a song we heard, or a book we read. It will hit our spirit and we will know it is Him speaking if we stay alert and aware, and don't block Him out by distractions and unbelief. We can't make decisions based on just our emotions. God gives us many gifts through His Spirit, but we have to seek Him to bring them into manifestation.

There are contrasts between walking by the flesh and walking by the Holy Spirit. We are told the difference between the two in Galatians 5:16, "But I say, walk and live (habitually) in the (Holy) Spirit (responsive to and controlled and guided by the Spirit); then you will certainly not gratify the cravings and desires of the flesh (of human nature without God). For the desires of the flesh are opposed to the (Holy) Spirit, and the (desires of the) Spirit are opposed to the flesh (godless human nature); for these are antagonistic with each other, so that you are not free but are prevented from doing what you desire to do. But if you are guided (led) by the (Holy) Spirit, you are not subject to the law. Now the doings (practices) of the flesh are clear (obvious); they are immorality, impurity, indecency, idolatry, sorcery, enmity, strife, jealousy, anger (ill temper), selfishness, divisions (dissensions), party spirit (factions, sects with peculiar opinions), heresies, envy, drunkenness, carousing, and the like. I warn you beforehand, just as I did previously, that those who do such things will not inherit the kingdom of God. But the work of the (Holy) Spirit (the work which this presence within accomplishes) is love, joy (gladness), peace, patience (an even temper, forbearance), kindness, goodness (benevolence), faithfulness, gentleness (meekness, humility), self-control (self-restraint), against such things there is no law (that can bring a charge). And those who belong to Christ Jesus (the Messiah) have crucified the flesh (the godless human nature) with its passions and appetites and desires. If we live by the (Holy) Spirit, let us also walk by the Spirit. (If by the Holy Spirit we have our life in God, let us go forward walking in line, our conduct controlled by the Spirit)."

The Holy Spirit is the One who empowers us and helps us to manifest these good characteristics so others can see the good fruits in our lives. It is not by our own works or will power. Not only is our life changed, but others will be drawn to God through the evidence of the Holy Spirit operating in us. You will always be like who you behold. That does not make us perfect. We will make mistakes and will need to constantly yield to His correction. When we blow it and fall down, we get up and brush the dirt off, and keep going forward learning from our mistakes.

The Holy Spirit is also our comforter. God's presence in our lives will comfort us when we are hurting. It is the peace we feel in spite of the pain. He will put us in remembrance of God's goodness no matter what trial we are going through. Jesus said in John 14: 25-26, "I have told you these things while I am still with you. But the Comforter, (Counselor, Helper, Intercessor, Advocate, Strengthener, Standby), the Holy Spirit, Whom the Father will send in My name [in My place, to represent Me and act on My behalf], He will teach you all things. And He will cause you to recall (will remind you of, bring to your remembrance) everything I have told you." Hebrews 2: 3-4, "How shall we escape (appropriate retribution) if we neglect and refuse to pay attention to such a great salvation (as it is now offered to us, letting it drift past us forever)? For it was declared at first by the Lord (Himself) and it was confirmed to us and proved to be real and genuine by those who personally heard (Him speak). Besides this evidence it was also established and plainly endorsed by God, who showed His approval of it by signs and wonders and various miraculous manifestations of (His) power and by imparting the gifts of the Holy Spirit (to the believers) according to His own will." It is a deception to think that the supernatural power of the Holy Spirit was only evident 2000 years ago.

The life changing power of the Holy Spirit is for today. Remember, the Bible says God is the same yesterday, today, and

The Holy Spirit

always. If you have a relationship with Jesus, you also have the Holy Spirit. We can tap into His anointing and our calling and gifts or we can restrict Him and ignore it. We can live with the purpose of only staying out of hell or we can live knowing that we have a purpose and a higher calling. To have faith is good, but to see results from it we must activate it. When we pray for something, often times we will be given an instruction from the Holy Spirit before we see the answer. It is following the instruction the Holy Spirit gives us out of obedience that brings us the results.

God gives us gifts through His Spirit to be used to bring Him glory. Whatever our gifting is will be used to help someone else and fulfill our destiny. He uses our arm as His arm and He stretches it out to hurting people. Just like someone has stretched their arm to reach us. If you ask Him, He will start to reveal what your gifts are.

In these prophetic dark times, He is using supernatural manifestations to draw His people to His Kingdom. It takes the supernatural signs, wonders, and miracles to get our attention, whether it is big or small. In a lot of cases it is the only way that some people will believe in Him.

1 Corinthians 12:1-11, "Now about the spiritual gifts (the special endowments of supernatural energy), brethren, I do not want you to be misinformed. You know that when you were heathen, you were led off after idols that could not speak [habitually] as impulse directed and whenever the occasion might arise. Therefore, I want you to understand that no one speaking under the power and influence of the [Holy] Spirit of God can [ever] say, Jesus be cursed! And no one can [really] say Jesus is [my] Lord, except by and under the power and influence of the Holy Spirit. Now there are distinctive varieties and distributions of endowments (gifts, extraordinary powers distinguishing certain Christians due to the divine grace operating in their souls by the Holy Spirit) and they vary, but the [Holy] Spirit remains the same. And there are distinctive varieties of service and ministration, but it is the same Lord [who is served]. And there are distinctive varieties of operation [of working to accomplish things], but it is the same God who inspires and energizes them all in all. But to each one is given the manifestation of the [Holy] Spirit [the evidence, the spiritual illumination of the Spirit] for good and profit.

To one is given in and through the [Holy] Spirit [the power to speak] a message of wisdom, and to another [the power to express] a word of knowledge and understanding, according to the same [Holy] Spirit; To another [wonder working] faith by the same [Holy] Spirit, to another the extraordinary powers of healing by the one Spirit. To another the working of miracles, to another prophetic insight (the gift of interpreting the divine will and purpose); to another the ability to discern and distinguish between [the utterances of true] spirits [and false ones], to another various kinds of [unknown tongues], to another the ability to interpret [such] tongues. All these [gifts, achievements, abilities] are inspired and brought to pass by one and the same [Holy] Spirit, Who apportions to each person individually [exactly] as He chooses."

God still uses apostles, prophets, and people who are anointed with healing in their hands, prophetic insight, and supernatural faith today.

Each one of us has natural gifts, talents, and abilities that God has given to us. Some people are extraordinarily gifted musically, with teaching, preaching, writing, with encouraging others; some have the gift of mercy, hospitality, and wisdom. Some are gifted for business, administration, missions; some are artistic, gifted in the ministry of helps, etc. We were each born with at least one, sometimes more. We are given these gifts by the Holy Spirit and not by our own merit, although it is up to us to discover and develop them. We are to gratefully use them to help others and not just for our own personal gain. Salvation and forgiveness come from His grace (a free gift) and not because we have done anything to earn or deserve it. Any gifting that comes from the Holy Spirit has the ultimate goal of bringing God the glory and bringing people face to face with Him. They are not to be misused.

Some people have no problems with the supernatural when it comes to various forms of witchcraft, psychics, horoscopes, objects that represent good luck, paranormal activities, and so forth; but think the church has gone crazy when you talk about the Holy Spirit moving supernaturally. Who do you think the author is of that distortion? Satan does not want us to have anything to do with the Holy Spirit and His supernatural manifestations. He does not care if we believe,

The Holy Spirit

even demons believe. He does not want the Christian advancing the kingdom of God by having signs, wonders, and miracles following them. We give the enemy a big enough headache just by spreading and sharing the gospel of Jesus Christ. Unfortunately, there have been too many people over the years that have misrepresented and discredited the gifts of the Holy Spirit and used them in a counterfeit way. There have been the false prophets and healers who were soliciting for the money or the fame. The Bible warned us about that. Matthew 7:15, "Beware of false prophets, who come to you dressed up as sheep, but inside they are devouring wolves." Therefore, a large portion of certain denominations as well as unbelievers have either made a mockery of it or are afraid of it. They doubt the authentic moving of the Holy Spirit. They believe that God can do miracles, but have a hard time recognizing that the Holy Spirit can bring the manifestation of them through and in our churches.

The Holy Spirit is the presence and manifestation of God. Not operating in any of the gifts of the Holy Spirit does not mean that He does not reside in you, because if you belong to Christ He does. We just limit Him and what He can do through us and for us in our lives. There will come a time when each of us will require supernatural help.

We should not be envious of the gift someone else has, but use the gifts we have been given. We are a body of believers and each part has a different function. When we unite and share our gifts, much can be accomplished for Christ and what He wants for His people on Earth. The greatest gift we can have is the gift of love towards other people. If we don't have love then the rest of the gifts are useless.

Religious doctrine has limited the operations of the Holy Spirit. A religious mind wants to keep God in their box, the way they think He should operate. That is why it is important to look to the Word to know the truth, because the truth will set your mind free. We complicate it too much. The odds are you have had some supernatural intervention or a miracle in your own life. You accepted it because it was in a certain setting or under certain circumstances. You can see the signs that the world is getting darker and our time is very short. There will be no human remedy for our situations.

We need a supernatural intervention. God is the author of miracles and the supernatural. The ministry of the Holy Spirit must be respected. Blasphemy against the Holy Spirit is the only unpardonable sin. Matthew 12:31, "Therefore I tell you, every sin and blasphemy (every evil, abusive, injurious speaking or indignity against sacred things) can be forgiven men, but blasphemy against the [Holy] Spirit shall not and cannot be forgiven."

John 6:2, "And a great crowd was following Him because they had seen the signs (miracles) which He [continually] performed upon those who were sick." John 6:14, "When the people saw the sign (miracle) that Jesus had performed, they began saying, Surely and beyond a doubt this is the Prophet Who is to come into the world!"

The Healing Power of God

The anointing God put on John Taylor was the anointing to pray for the sick and hurting. This is his calling and his ministry. John is not a Pastor, he is a servant of the Lord Jesus Christ. He knows God's inner voice (Holy Spirit) and he responds to it. God sets up divine appointments for him and puts people in his path.

We can consume the scriptures that relate to healing and have it so established in our heart and mind that it will produce faith to bring it into manifestation. Romans 10:17, "So faith comes by hearing [what was told], and what was heard comes by the preaching [of the message that came from the lips] of Christ (the Messiah Himself)." Faith comes by hearing the word of God. Hebrews 11: 1 says, "NOW FAITH is the assurance (the confirmation, the title deed) of the things [we] hope for, being the proof of things [we] do not see and the conviction of their reality [faith perceiving as real fact what is not revealed to the senses]." There is a proverb that states, "As a man thinks, a man is." Words we speak are powerful and create an effect. God used words and spoke everything into creation. This pertains to our thoughts as well. Thoughts are powerful and create a reaction. Even secular psychologists will tell you that. It is a spiritual law and a natural law. It can affect our physical and emotional health. That is why meditating on scriptures can renew our mind. Doctors have done studies on this. Negative and toxic thoughts can affect your emotional and physical health. They can make you sick and even cause cancer. The opposite is true as well. Positive, faith filled thoughts and words are healing to the soul, body, and mind. What we think about and meditate on is essential to our well-being. That is why supernatural healing usually follows a word or message we have heard. It penetrates your heart and supernatural faith springs forth to receive what has been spoken.

Jesus and His disciples preached the kingdom of God first, and THEN brought healing to people. Luke 9: 1-2, "Then Jesus called together the twelve (apostles) and gave them power and authority over all demons and to cure diseases, and He sent them out to preach the kingdom of God and to bring healing."

Faith is also activated through prayer. We are hearing our petition or someone praying on our behalf go straight to the throne room of God. God never intended for us to deal with sickness and disease. That was a result of sin entering the world. All of the other curses came with it. If we belong to God's kingdom and not the world's kingdom we are no longer living under the curse.

Everything we receive from God is by faith and His grace. We believe in Him even though we can't physically see Him. Romans 8:16, "The Holy Spirit Himself testifies together with our own spirit, (assuring us) that we are children of God." Before we sit in a chair we believe it will support us without asking it to prove itself first. If you find it hard to believe in something that you cannot physically see, ask God to reveal Himself to you in a personal way and He will.

Jesus desires to heal us from our sufferings. No one suffered more than He did. He understands and has compassion and mercy for us. Hebrews 2:18, "For because He Himself (in His humanity) has suffered in being tempted (tested and tried), He is able (immediately) to run to the cry (assist, relieve) those who are being tempted and tested and tried (and who therefore are being exposed to suffering)." He wants us to run to Him for whatever need we have. Matthew 11:28 "Come to Me, all you who labor and are heavy-laden and overburdened, and I will cause you to rest. [I will ease and relieve your souls]." He is simply looking for those who will seek Him with faith believing He is Who He says He is, and He does what He says He will do.

Healing and restoration in a believer's life is biblical. Matthew 4:23, "And He went about all Galilee, teaching in their synagogues and preaching the good news (gospel) of the kingdom, and healing every disease and every weakness and infirmity among the people."

Our faith and the prayers of faith with other believers are powerful. Jesus gave us authority by using His Name in prayer to impose God's plans for us over the purposes Satan has planned for us. James 4:16, "Confess to one another therefore your faults (your slips, your false steps, your offenses, your sins) and pray (also) for one another, that you may be healed and restored (to a spiritual tone of mind and heart). The earnest (heartfelt, continued) prayer of a righteous man makes tremendous power available [dynamic in its working]."

Never underestimate the power of prayer and faith. Luke 8:43-48, "And a woman who had suffered from a flow of blood for twelve years and had spent all her living upon physicians, and could not be healed by anyone, came up upon Him and touched the fringe of His garment, and immediately her flow of blood ceased. And Jesus said, who is it who touched me? When all were denying it, Peter and those who were with Him said, Master, the multitudes surround You and press You on every side! But Jesus said, someone did touch me; for I perceived that [healing] power has gone forth from me. And when the woman saw that she had not escaped unnoticed, she came up trembling, and falling down before Him, she declared in the presence of all the people for what reason she had touched Him and how she had been instantly cured. And He said to her, Daughter, your faith (your confidence and trust in me) has made you well! Go (enter) into peace (untroubled, undisturbed well-being)."

There are several things worth pointing out in that scripture. First, that woman "pressed" (diligently) past the crowds and actively did what she could to be "near" (close to) Him. She wanted and went after her healing. She was not passive about it. Second, her faith in Him was activated when she "reached" (sought after) and "touched" (made personal contact with) Him. She was focused on Him alone and not the crowds and what they would think of her. Third, she also "declared" (voiced her faith and praise) with her mouth what He had done and gave Him the credit. If we all went after Jesus like that with that kind of faith and perseverance, just think what He would do for us in all areas of our life. Faith is not passive. Faith requires something from us. It is a verb and not a noun. God did not part the Red Sea until Moses stepped out in faith and put his foot on it.

Just as faith produces results, so does unbelief and fear. If we doubt and have unbelief, our prayers are blocked. If our fear has grown stronger than our faith, we are paralyzed. Fear has the same energy as faith, but moves us in the opposite direction. We all have our fears, but it is when fear has consumed our mind that it blocks our faith.

God deals with each of us differently, according to what He knows is best for us. As you have read, frequently healing is instant. Other times it is progressive. He works on us and in us over a period of time before we see results. He is doing a work inside of us. He wants us to trust Him every step of the way and this builds our faith and our ability to persevere, and our desire to seek Him for who He is and not just what He can do.

God Uses Doctors

God will use the hands of doctors as His Hands to heal us. He is the one who has given them the intelligence, skills and wisdom. We can't limit God and dictate to Him how to answer us. He has the ultimate wisdom and His ways are not our ways. He uses doctors every day to answer prayers. For some people their expectation in their prayers is that God will move through doctors whether that is through conventional, alternative, or holistic medicine. Not all people believe that God can heal in any other way.

Some infirmities (illnesses) are passed down from generation to generation, and others are a result of our life style choices and our environment. He may give us an instruction to change some things in how we live, think, and take care of ourselves. Jesus gave a sick man an instruction in John 5: 5-8, "There was a certain man there who had suffered with a deep-seated and lingering disorder for thirty-eight years. When Jesus noticed him lying there [helpless], knowing that he had already been a long time in that condition, He said to him, 'Do you want to become well?' ['Are you really in earnest about getting well?'] The invalid answered, 'Sir, I have nobody when the water is moving to put me into the pool; but while I am trying to come [into it] myself, someone else steps down ahead of me.' Jesus said to him, 'Get up! Pick up your bed (sleeping pad) and walk!'" Jesus gave him an instruction and it sounds like this man had excuses that kept him in that condition for 38 years. If you think about that scripture, it can also mean that there was no one who shared the gospel with him. The Holy Spirit is always moving, but He needs us to share our faith with others. We have to do our part, and then let Him do His part while trusting Him, and leaving the consequences to Him.

The first miracle Jesus preformed on Earth was turning water into wine for a seven day wedding feast and celebration. He gave an instruction first that He needed pots filled with water. His own mother knew the importance of the instruction and told the servers, "Do what He tells you to do." The church is instructed to pray for the sick. In the Greek language, the word sick means powerless. That is why our obedience to all of His instructions is vital to seeing His glory (goodness) manifested in our lives. He gave us a free will to make our own choices, but He can also redeem our bad choices and give us a brand new start.

Illness can be a result from us not listening to His warnings about doing certain things. He was trying to prevent it instead of us dealing with the consequences of it. He wants the best for us. When sin entered the world through Adam and Eve's disobedience, illness and death entered as well. This was not God's original plan for us, but Adam and Eve were given a free will too. They were deceived because Satan spoke to them and said what God said to them was not true. He roams the Earth trying to convince all of us of this regarding everything God has said. Everything that proceeds from God's mouth is for our benefit. Satan has fooled people in to believing that the world's way of doing things is the right way.

Jesus says in Matthew 7:13-14, "Enter through the narrow gate; for wide is the gate and spacious and broad is the way that leads away to destruction, and many are those who are entering through it. But the gate is narrow (contradicted by pressure) and the way is straightened and compressed that leads away to life, and few are those who find it."

God is omniscient (knowing all things, having universal or complete knowledge). That is why we won't have all the answers in this life for the people who have been prayed for and were not healed, or they died suddenly or tragically. Some people refer to death as one of His answers to healing, being in a place where there is no more pain. He knows the future and we do not. In this world He does call some people home early for reasons that we will not understand, but He does. It does not mean He loves one person more than another. He is no respecter of persons and He loves us all the same. He may know in certain situations that a person He calls home, may result in the impacting of many other lives. I am aware of many times after someone has died, it has brought other people to Him who may not have turned to Him otherwise. He may know a person's future and what their choices and decisions may be, that they would turn away from their faith and God and lose their soul. Like John Taylor said, He would rather lose a child and know that child is with Jesus, than to raise that child and lose him or her to hell. This is true for adults as well.

Hell is just as real as Heaven. This does not mean that God ever puts illness or tragedy on us; that is against His nature. The enemy wants to take us out prematurely and he succeeds at it. This is true with believers and non-believers. That is why it is important that we pray constantly over ourselves and loved ones.

As long as we are on Earth, none of us are immune to suffering. He knows the past, present, and future of everyone. One thing we are promised if we are in relationship with Him, is that all things (even the bad) will eventually work out for our good; if we persevere, don't lose faith or hope, and finish running our race with Him to the end.

We are commanded to pray always without ceasing. We are promised that He hears our prayers. We must keep hate, intentional sin, resentments, lust, jealousy, greed, idolatry, and unforgiveness out of our life so our prayers are not hindered. We can only do this with His help and grace. Grace is His supernatural empowerment that He gives us to live this way. We can't do it by our flesh or our own works.

Forgiving other people is imperative to having our prayers answered. Again, forgiveness is the whole message of the cross. We can still believe and see that miracles happen every day despite all the bad things we see around us. For some unbelievers, witnessing a miracle is the only reason they will ever come to believe that God is real, alive and active.

Science and medicine have been baffled about events that have no explanation other than divine, supernatural intervention. Science tells us in general it does not believe in miracles because its study relies on natural laws, and miracles to scientists are not natural. God however is above the natural. He is a supernatural God and He deals in the supernatural and that is exactly what miracles are. . .they are supernatural. In fact, in a study of 1,000 doctors, it was found as many as 77 percent believed in miracles. Clearly without it being stated, they had seen things that were beyond their comprehension, their study, etc. If we were to look back on our own lives, I think you would find occasions where something has happened that was unexplainable; that the word coincidence or luck had no bearing on what happened. Jesus Himself said in John 14, that if we had faith in Him and believed in the things He had done that we would do the same and even greater, because He was going to the Father. After He died and went to the Father, The Holy Spirit was sent to the Earth shortly after, on the day of Pentecost. Now either Jesus was a liar or He was telling the truth and we know He was not a liar. It is important to study the scriptures so we will know the truth ourselves. Therefore, if you act on the truth no matter how silly you think you look, you may well be the miracle in someone's life.

The simple act of praying with them for healing, or the laying on of hands is not restricted. Nowhere does it say that this scripture is the province only of those whom are pastors, evangelists, prophets, etc. He answers our prayers in His timing and according to what we need. If the God who so touched us as we were born again reduced us to tears in gratitude, do you not think He would want to reduce us to tears in thanks for a miracle. You see in both cases it is about giving Him the glory. . .firstly for being born again and becoming a new creation and then secondly. . .for doing something with that new creation. For some if that means going home to be with Him, then we are eternally thankful. Just think about it for a moment. . .*eternity*. . .that is a miracle in itself.

A quote from T. David Sustar's book, *The Holy Spirit in Perspective*,"Miracles are the power of God operating by the Spirit of God in and through the church of God. They usually manifest in an unexpected manner and with a special intensity. Miracles are like fingers pointing to God and Christ, drawing people to them in reverence and awe."

Miracles manifest in numerous ways besides physical healing. They can manifest in any area of your life. . .in your finances, relationships, past hurts, on your job, your heart's desires, even on a beloved pet. God's mercy has no boundaries. God cares about every area of our life. Look how He has moved in national disasters. There are countless stories of life saving miracles.

It is the goodness of God that draws people to Him. He is a good God in the midst of an evil world. I hope this leaves you with hope in whatever situation you find yourself in today. If you have lost hope, call on the name of Jesus and He will never leave you nor forsake you or leave you without help. There are thousands of promises in the Bible that are ours for the taking. We have to read them, believe them, and put our voice in prayer to them. There is power in just speaking and declaring God's word.

When we pray our words it moves the heart of God, but when we pray His Word back to Him it moves the Hand of God. Matthew 10:20, "For it is not you who are speaking, but the Spirit of your Father speaking through you." Isaiah 55:11, "So shall My word that goes forth out of My mouth: it shall not return to Me void [without producing any effect, useless] but is shall accomplish that which I please and purpose, and it shall prosper in the thing for which it was sent." He calls it our sword over the enemy's tactics against us and it is sharper than a two edged sword. God asks us to put Him in remembrance of His Word. I don't think it is because He forgets it, but He knows we need to speak and declare it to manifest His will for us in the situations that we need intervention and revelation.

The Bible is not just a book to be read, it is like a bag of seeds. When we find a scripture that pertains to our situations and we stand on that promise in prayer consistently, we will reap a harvest from it and see answers manifest. It is what we say and do consistently that brings results.

The enemy wants to immobilize us in our pain and keep us contained so we don't move forward to the better things God has for us. We have to fight in prayer without wavering. Satan will come and try to steal that word from our heart and wants us to give up. Praying is warfare and you don't stop until the battle is won.

God's Word is our GPS system, the direction we need is hidden inside those pages. It is not a name it and claim it message, it is praying down His perfect will for us. Declaring His Word will give us the faith that our heart needs to believe all things are possible with God, even the supernatural miracle of healing in body, mind, and soul. It renews our mind to think like He thinks. What is impossible for us is not impossible for Him. He is the God of hope.

Psalm 119:116, "Uphold me according to Your promise, that I may live; and let me not be put to shame in my hope!"

Matthew 19:26, "But Jesus looked at them and said, with men this is impossible, but all things are possible with God."

Jeremiah 32:27, "Behold, I am the Lord, the God of all flesh; is there anything too hard for Me?"

About John Taylor

My dad, John A Taylor, married Ruby Jewel Causey. They lived on the outskirts of Port Arthur, Texas. They did not have much, no radio, not even electricity. They did have a fine wood burning stove. Water came from a cistern (big water tank) that came through the gutters that drained into it from the eves of the house.

After my dad, Bud (nickname) went to work, momma would lie across the bed and there wasn't that much for her to do. Therefore, she would lie across the bed and pray for a baby girl because she was lonesome. One day she was lying there praying and a voice spoke to her, "Would you take a boy?" Momma said, "What?" She heard the voice again, "Would you take a boy? We will give you a boy." Momma replied, "I will take a boy!" About nine or ten months later, here I came. Momma was never bored or lonesome again.

I was five years old when my father was killed at what was known then to be the Texaco Refinery. The next year the house burned to the ground with no insurance and then hard times set in. My mother raised her two boys and three first cousins. My brother Kenneth was born two years behind me.

When I was twenty-eight years old, the church I grew up in was divided. I walked up one time and took the microphone from the Pastor and preached my first sermon about division. The whole church emptied into the altar. The devil attacked me after that and I did not preach another sermon for forty-one years. Then the Lord changed my life and gave me another chance, and I have been a prayer warrior ever since. Satan is still trying to stop me, but I am on full alert and watch. The closer I get to Jesus the stronger I get.

I went to work for a dollar a day at a service station when I was eleven years old, fixing flat tires. I did not know the day would come when that simple skill would help me feed my family when I was twenty years old.

I married young for all the wrong reasons. Life from there is a story all of its own having nothing to do with the Lord's work. The years from there would make a book in itself, things I wished had not of happened. I had the spirit of stupid all over me.

When someone does wrong there are two choices. Learn from your mistakes or continue down the primrose path to hell. We can turn our bad history experiences into opportunities to help others. Some times what not to do is just as important as what you do!

In 1995, I won 4 State championships in competitive trail. That is over land on horseback. In 1999, I won another 4 State championships and the points were so high that I won Nationals also. I had planned to do that after I retired. I had a horse trailer that would haul three horses with full living quarters and air conditioning. It cost me $31,000.00 dollars. Now it sits with weeds growing around it.

I had two walls full of trophies and plaques. I took all of them down except for one. I put them in boxes and stored them in the tack room. I sold all of the horses except for Warrior (seen on cover) and one mare. I have not ridden a horse in months. Why? Because I have turned my life over to the Lord Jesus and no trophy or win of any kind, satisfies me like it does when the Holy Spirit shows up and grants the prayer for whoever I am praying for.

Then my wife and I decided to do better. We started going to church. We encountered the Holy Spirit and our life would never be the same again.

There are things in this book that addresses the supernatural that only the Father, Son, and Holy Spirit could do; from my trip to Heaven's Gate, to the multiplication of the anointing oil in the bottle (that I always carry in my pocket), including the many healings and salvations I have seen in my life. I give all the praise and glory to the Lord.

My whole ministry is based on Matthew: 22: 37-38. It is about loving the Lord with all of your heart and mind and loving your neighbor as yourself.

I can say without a doubt that every day is Christmas now.

Word from the Co-Author

John Taylor is in the process of changing my life through God who put him in my path. In 2007, the Lord told me through an apostle that I was a scribe and He wanted me to write. I was very surprised by this because I have only written thoughts in my private journals. I did not think I was qualified so I just put it in the back of my mind. In January 2011, I was fasting and praying about another concern. During the fast the Lord did not speak to me in regards to what I was praying about. He knew He had my full attention that month. So, He yelled it at me this time in my spirit that He wanted me to write. When I finally said yes, God lined up John and all the resources that I would need and put them in my lap. John's testimonies are incredible and need to be told. The Lord has told me several times since 2007 that, "The Spirit of the Lord God is upon me, because the Lord has anointed and qualified me to preach the Gospel of good tidings to the meek, the poor, and afflicted; He has sent me to bind up and heal the brokenhearted, to proclaim liberty to the [physical and spiritual] captives and the opening of the prison and of the eye to those who are bound." Isaiah 61:1.

I am His messenger through writing. God does not call the qualified, but He qualifies the called. Certificates and degrees are not required. He can use anyone. All of His disciples and followers while on this Earth, had their inadequacies and weaknesses, but He used them the most because those are the people we can relate to. He calls people who have been through some stuff so we can help others who are going through the same thing. He called me to write because I have been afflicted, brokenhearted, meek, poor, and a spiritual and physical captive. Not because I am anyone special. God looks for those who are willing to be used to help set His captives free. I have been through much in my life and God has delivered me from so much. He has done one miracle after another in my life and He has saved my life several times, even in my mother's womb. The doctor suggested that my mom should consider terminating me because of pregnancy complications. The doctor was concerned about her life and said I would probably not survive, but she said no. My mom asked people to pray for me. When I was born the hospital called me the "Miracle baby."

When I began writing this book, my mother was hanging on for her life in the hospital. I asked John Taylor and others to pray for her. Her cardiologist told her that she would probably need heart surgery, but she decided to wait a month before making that decision. When she came back to see him and had more tests, her results showed that she did not need the surgery after all. Her heart had improved because God had intervened.

God supernaturally saved me from death several times as an adult as well. One day I will write and share my story. I do know

Word from the Co-Author

about miracles. I have seen and experienced them. It is an honor and a privilege to write about the miracles that follow John Taylor's ministry when he prays. I am humbled that the Lord and John picked me. All the stories you have read are John Taylor's stories. I am just the messenger. These stories come from his journals and I love his Texas style and humor. John is authentic. God gets the credit and glory for this book and John is His faithful servant.

I have seen God's grace and mercy over and over again in my life. I have been blessed and forgiven more times than I can count.

I believe in supernatural miracles and the power of the Holy Spirit. The Lord woke me up early one morning and spoke to my spirit as I was writing this book. He said it is going to take the supernatural manifestations in these prophetic dark times to draw people back to Him. Too many people have let their hearts become hard and cold from a cruel world and disappointments.

John has become a friend and prayer warrior for me as well. I have the utmost respect for this man's heart, character, integrity and credibility. I am glad that I finally said yes to writing instead of doubting it. The enemy reminds me of what my faults are and of my past mistakes. I took a leap of faith and opened up my ears to hear who God says I am and what He can do through me. What I could not do on my own. I decided to write for the Lord by faith. Like Joyce Meyer says, "I am not yet where I want to be, but thank God I am not where I used to be."

This book is God's book and the message in this book is for you. The person who is hurting, needs faith, salvation, hope, or for the person who needs a miracle. I pray that the Holy Spirit speaks to you, touches your heart, shows you truth and gives you a bigger revelation of Who He Is. I also pray that all of us in these hard times will never stop believing in and praying for miracles by the grace of Jesus Christ. John Taylor desires that this book will leave you with hope and healing.

I am thankful for John Taylor, Apostle Ronnie Adkins, Dr. Jonie' Dodgens, Pastor Lisa Satterberg, Cyndi Walter and Dr. Joe Fawcett (www.DrJoeFawcett.com), who believed in me and encouraged me to write.

I want to thank Celebration Church of Fresno, California, Pastor Randy Hand and Pastor Damon Thompson, for teaching me the difference between religion and a relationship with Him. I am thankful for their teaching and inspiration that led me to know God at a deeper level.

I also want to thank my precious daughters Kara Meyer and Kailee White.

Robin White, Co-Author

About the Cowboy, Horse and the Cross

This is the story behind the picture that is seen on the cover of this book. It was taken in 2006, and has been uplifting for many people, especially single mothers who have children. I believe that God decided to anoint this picture. Many people have broken out in chills, some cried, others tingled. One young lady had asked me to pray for her and her children. As I was leaving, I handed her a framed copy of this picture. She started to fall down to the pavement and I caught her. This was confirmation to me that the Holy Spirit was using this picture. It is something that God is using to uplift His people. Sometimes He sends me with a prayer and a picture.

It all started after the ACLU sent lawyers after a man in California. He was a man who had a rather large cross in his pasture near the highway. People would say "Go to the cross and turn right or left." Or they would say "Go one mile past the cross." GO TO THE CROSS, that is the part the ACLU did not like. They declared it a State Monument and shut the ACLU down on this matter.

In 2006, when that story was unfolding on television, I sat there and was mad until they said it was a State Monument. As I watched this, things began to unfold in my mind. I had always wanted one in my yard, but did not want to be associated with the KKK.

I know now that the Lord was showing me in my mind, do it this way. I then started dragging down timbers and painted it red for the blood and put the Star of David on the top. I then wrote across the cross "THANK YOU JESUS." No one could doubt my intent.

My daughter-in-law Jamie took the picture of me, Taylor (my grandson), Warrior, and the cross photo.

John with baby Taylor

Taylor was born one week after the hurricane Rita. They lived with us for the first eighteen months of Taylor's life. It took that long to get the house fixed.

When I decided to do *The Cowboy, Horse and Cross* picture, Jamie took to it immediately. I did not feel good about it at first, but the picture turned out great. I said, "Jamie, let's do something different." I grabbed my grandson Taylor. Jamie took the picture again and this time it felt right! (Divine moment)

I had no idea how right I was. . .from the first one I had framed for my mother, people were having reactions to it as I mentioned. People have tried to buy it and I tell them, "It is not for sale." There are thousands of them now in the States, and that does not count the evangelists who have carried it into the Russian Ukraine. I understand they like anything western over there.

Most of the picture is not about me. . .the baby Taylor represents you, your children, even me and all God's children. Somehow, even though I am retired, God has provided the money. I have been able to give 5,000 plus away framed and that doesn't count what went into the Russian Ukraine. It feels good to me when people are encouraged by it. I hear there is one on the table in front of the pulpit in a church in Arkansas. Hankmer Community Church west of Winnie, Texas asked me for one. As I write this, there are four churches that I know of that are using it. The Lord is using it.

For a long time I was worried because I was in the picture. Then a word from the Lord came to me and said, "Don't worry about it!" Most men would not have their picture taken bowing before a cross anyway.

There are many stories about the stallion's name, Warrior. A stripper came to my barn to see him. She had seen his picture somewhere. I cannot always explain how God works. Ten minutes after her arrival, she had her head in my chest. The Holy Spirit had rained down on her and months later she was still free of drugs and alcohol. PRAISE GOD!

God bless you and yours. We will pray for you. I am not a pastor or a preacher. I have just sold out to the Lord since 2002. That is when I started to see miracles happen. This picture went around the world. . .so far twice. It is all GOD! There are a lot of testimonies from this picture from single mothers and their babies.

P.S. Thank you ACLU! Now the Lord has sent the horse and the cross picture around the world by satellite, twice! Soon it will go into the Middle East, Kenya and the rest of Africa, the Netherlands as well. I recently found out that it is also in the Arkansas prison system. The inmates are making wood carvings from it.

Thank you Lord for using the horse and the Cross, and Taylor Tot all around the world. God bless,

John and Connie Taylor, Taylor Tot & Warrior

To contact the Ministry of John Taylor for prayer, a CD of *Make My Life a Bible*, or a DVD of his television interview with Tommy Thomas, please contact:

John Taylor
P.O Box 644
Kountze, TX 77625
Email: MakeMyLifeABible@wildblue.net
Web site: www.MakeMyLifeABible.com

Taylor Tot